Adventures At The Outer Limits Of Consciouness

Keith Scott-Mumby

Published by:
NewReality, Inc
1090 Victorine Rd.
Livermore, CA 94551
877-828-3644

10 9 8 7 6 5 4 3 2 1

A catalogue record for this book is available from the British Library
and from the Library of Congress, Washington

ISBN-13: 978-1-4507-5818-5

Printed in USA by
Bang Printing, Brainerd, MN

Cover design and layout by Dragos Balasoiu (dragosb.com/design)

Dedicated to my beloved wife Vivien and to that wonderful patient who offered to show me fairies the day before she was grabbed and put away as insane.

"This is writing of such power, depth and beauty that it makes *The Celestine Prophecy* read like a bus timetable."

—Adryenn Ashley, WowIsMe.net

"The stream of knowledge is heading towards a non-mechanical reality; the universe begins to look more like a great thought than a great machine"

-Sir James Jeans, The Mysterious Universe, 1938 (reprint).

"A genuine theory of everything must explain not only how our universe came into being, but also why it is the only type of universe that there could have been - why there could only be one set of laws. This goal I believe to be illusory"

-"No Faith in the Grand Theory", Russell Stannard, The Times (London) 13 Nov 1989

The English word 'fairy' comes to us, via the Old French faerie, from the Latin fata, meaning 'fate'. This means the roots of the present word are with the classical Greek Fates, who were believed to control the destiny of the human race.

Contents

I. The Old People

The Celts have always known the fairy folk and held them in honor long after the rest of the world dismissed such notions as mere childhood fantasy. The Gaelic word for fairy is *Sithe* (pronounced *shee*), a sound like the whisper of a zephyr in the long, bent hillside grasses. The fairies themselves like to be known as the Old People.

My first encounter was on Skye, a fact which will come as no surprise to many. On that mystical isle, where the weeping clouds of the Atlantic have made their chosen home, the Other World is very close; it hangs there like a damp veil. One gets the feeling that there are voices and people just beyond the curtain, not in this world, and yet so close that it would take only the slightest motion to reach out and touch them. The land is haunted by wandering spirits that have perhaps lost the will to leave such a lovely place; their sighs are in the very air.

The traditions of magic have clung here throughout the centuries. Did not the Great McLeod meet with a fairy and she gave him a flag to protect his clan? Twice it has been unfurled in battle; on both occasions the chieftain's army prevailed. It can be seen today, framed and hung above the mantel shelf in Dunvegan Castle, ancestral home of the McLeods. The Fairy Bridge, where the meeting took place, is still marked on the Ordnance

Survey map, though it no longer carries traffic; the stream of cars and tourist coaches rushes past less than a hundred yards to the south and few people, these days, even know it is there.

So entrenched has been the islanders' belief in the supernatural that in 1870 there was an attempt to drag the loch at Suardal, near Broadford, trying to capture the famed *Each Uisge* or water horse. As everyone knows, any mortal unlucky enough to be siezed by this wicked monster and thrown on its back as it dives under the water will never be seen again. *Uisge*, pronounced *Ooshka*, means water in Gaelic and has been corrupted to give us the word "whisky", a drink known fondly as *water of life* in these parts! Even as I write, I am looking at an old faded photograph taken on the day of the attempt to capture the water horse. Men and women stand posed solemnly for the camera in Victorian costume. It seems incredible that what would elsewhere be dismissed as Mediaeval superstition could be taken so seriously in Britain, well into the modern industrial age.

Every courageous soul photographed that day is long dead. The little church of *Chille Chroisd* (Christ Church) where they all prayed for strength and protection in the face of evil is now in ruins, the roof gone and the winds of time whistle through its sad walls. On a summer's day it is yet a pretty place and some visitors, rushing to distant Elgol, may stop and take a photograph or two and wonder about the names and identities depicted by the tombstones.

But on a November night, when the clouds obscure moon and stars, it is very different. I have been there in the darkest dark, on the wild heath between the church and loch, and felt my blood curdle with fear. For that is the time evil Ludag is abroad, the one-legged goblin, looking for victims to kick to death.

There can be no question that Skye, even at the passing of the millennium, was a place where the Old Order meets the new; sometimes the turbulent eddies can be strongly felt.

2. Night On A Bare Mountain

How can I give you a clearer picture of the strange mixture of magic and reality which is to be found on the Isle Of Skye? Maybe, if you come with me on one of my adventures, I will be able to enthrall you with the weird and wonderful that is to be encountered in this corner of Scotland.

Find me sitting on a rocky mountain-top, alone and in the dark, with plenty of time to ask myself questions. Nothing too deep; just immediate down-to-earth enquiries such as — what fit of madness brought me here? Was there any way to stop shivering? Would I die of hypothermia?

The idea of spending the night on a Cuillin peak had haunted me for years, ever since reading Seton Gordon, in his wonderful book *"The Charm Of Skye"*, describe a soft summer night spent on the peak of Sgurr Dearg (the Red Peak).

To do the same myself someday had become one of those lingering ambitions that nag away at the back of the mind, unfulfilled. The wish became even more intense, a longing almost, when in later years I read the autobiography of the twentieth-century Sioux medicine man John Fire, known also by his Lakota name of Lame Deer.

Lame Deer was prepared for his calling by being left alone on a mountain top, without food or water, to face rattlesnakes, bears, cougars and, worst of all, his inner fears. From him I received kinship with a fellow medicine man and the fire of enquiry that never leaves a soul, once implanted.

The years passed. I worked in the accident and emergency room (ER) of a busy metropolitan hospital, south of the border in Manchester, England. I saw life, death (lots of that) and the indomitable human spirit and learned it is not the same as our temporal, fleshly life. The honorable calling of a healer, to me, was my chosen pathway to goodness.

Then, almost by accident, I found myself in Glenbrittle with a day to spare. This glen sits nestled under the grand peaks, right on the ocean's shore. It was the main climbing centre for the south and western end of the horseshoe-shaped range of mountains called, ominously, the Black Cuillins (pronounced coolins).

The midsummer weather was gloriously hot and I realized the moment would never be better. So after a good supper and a bottle, with Lame Deer firmly in mind, I registered with the Glenbrittle warden and found myself setting out up the west ridge of Sgurr Dearg as the sun threw long shadows across the heather in front of me.

"The official line," said the warden, as I told him what I proposed to do, "is to tell you not to go alone." But he added with a wink, "Don't quote me, but I wish I was doing the same! In my day we did things that would seem foolhardy now, just to test ourselves."

That was the point really, I wanted to test myself.

Nothing breeds rash enthusiasm as readily as crass ignorance, and I had plenty of that! My climbing experience in these peaks was limited to say the least. If I had learned anything on my infrequent visits, it was that the Cuillin are forbidding and dangerous to foolish and unwary amateurs such as myself. The trouble was, once started, to have second thoughts—even on the grounds of common sense—would be a failure of nerve. I had to go through with it, or lose my self esteem.

Not that there was anything to be afraid of at first. The upward toil needed all my concentration. Despite the late evening hour, the air was hot and heavy. It wasn't long before I was gasping with effort and pouring sweat. Skye is a place to be fit, not get fit, I told myself, trying to remember if I was being witty or whether I had read that somewhere.

However, my non-optimum physical condition brought its own strange reward. Instead of slogging onwards, face to the mountain, the frequent necessary stops provided ample opportunity to turn and gaze behind me at the view. Slowly the panorama of the isle-encircled sea called the Minch grew, like a developing photographic print. As the sunset and the sea glowed, that wild and wonderful expanse of islands and water began to look like lily pads floating in a vast pool of liquid gold.

It was breathtaking . . . and I mean no pun on the state of my heaving lungs!

At about two and a half thousand feet came the first rush of night air. As it struck the narrowing ridge it let out an awful moan, like a cry of torment. It was a creepy sound and I shivered, though perspiration was still trickling from my forehead. The last five hundred feet were tricky, as on so many demanding peaks. There were precipices to either side and I thought of nothing except where to place my feet safely in the gathering dusk.

By ten o'clock I had reached the top. It was gloomy but the light had not faded entirely. I looked around nervously. The ring of shattered peaks looked gaunt and eerie; it was an unholy place to spend the night alone. I was having strong second thoughts but there was no going back; it would be dark in less than an hour.

Once I gained the summit, the first task was to find some shelter. Anyone who knows the Cuillin ridge will know there isn't a comfortable spot to sit anywhere on the cracked and broken rock. It seemed hopeless and in the end I settled for an awkward niche against the wind. It was less than two feet deep and I huddled into it, thinking of the hours of darkness ahead.

I was soon shivering with cold and the prospects seemed bleak; I had no sleeping bag and only a casual jacket, which didn't even zip right to the collar. For the first time I began thinking about survival. Had I miscalculated and placed myself in great danger? Or was I simply in for a wretched night of cold and discomfort for my fool-hardiness? I was uncertain and genuinely apprehensive.

The real danger, I told myself, was probably not from conditions as they existed but from developing bad weather. Cloud seemed to be building up to the south, banks of it hovering over the island of Rhum on a level with myself. If it surrounded me and turned foul I knew I would be in trouble. I could not get down safely in the dark. With unfamiliar ground and yawning precipices on all sides, even to try would be folly.

I had no control over what happened now and simply resigned myself to whatever was in store. Instead of worrying I turned my mind to the view. Even in the fast fading light there was plenty to see. A few scattered lights marked hamlets in the distance They were so far away and below my perch that I felt isolated and cut off from the rest of the human race. One by one lighthouses winked into life, friendly and reassuring. I tried to make them out from the map but it was too dark to read.

Slowly the sun's afterglow moved northwards. Occasional car headlamps crawled against the landscape, immeasurably slowed down by scale and distance, like insects exploring a slab of burnt cake. These contacts with safety diminished, one by one. There is nothing much to do on Skye after dark and I suppose by midnight most people had taken to their beds.

In a tiny scrape in the bony rock, in the deep velvet night at three thousand feet, I looked down on the world below and felt about as remote from human life as anyone can feel, while yet within the borders of an industrialized country.

Then, at about 1.30 a.m. the clouds swept aside. The moon sailed gaily into view and stars pricked out. Almost at once I felt better. High overhead was Vega, the blue and beautiful gem of Lyra, queen of the summer skies. I realized suddenly I was safe after all! I could allow myself to laugh at my earlier fears and did so long and loud. It warmed me heartily and even the cold seemed less.

For the first time I stood up and looked out from my eagle's eyrie. Through the sparkling sharp air I could see fantastic forms, a landscape carved from blackened rock, crags and promontories thrown up, separated by plunging chasms. The sea sprawled below like liquid pewter in the white moonlight. It was an indescribable majesty, perspectives magnified by the dark. I tried to imagine a time when the earth was young, before any man lived, and thought just for a moment I succeeded in getting a glimpse of what it must have been like.

The temperature fell inexorably. Despite the time of year, snow was evident at this level and its presence did nothing to sustain the inner glow. At times the shivering became so violent I feared I would pull a muscle. A few hours of that and I knew I would be physically exhausted In the heat of the evening I had underestimated the bitter night cold and cursed myself loudly.

Inevitably, there came a low point. Stressed by the anxiety that there could be no rescue, hungry due to lack of food and considerably exhausted by the unceasing violence of shivering, I passed into a dreamy state in which reality became blurred. It was then I saw the most awesome vision, just the sheer size of which was an amazement and surprise.

In the valley immediately to the east of me, sitting on the lower slopes of the mountain, I saw a creature that was three thousand feet high, its head level with the nearest mountain tops. It had a huge ram-like head with horns, but a human form, with hands and feet. On its lap was a carcass of some kind, which I could not identify.

I was not afraid, which ought to have surprised me, but it didn't—I suppose this "thing" could have reached me in one huge stride. But at some level I knew I was not threatened by the apparition, whatever it was. Instead, it seemed that a door had deliberately opened to another reality and I was meant to catch a glimpse of what was inside.

Trying to remember the events of that night I now doubt I even saw things with the eyes of my body. It is hard to be certain of the experience, except for one other impression. The creature let out an almighty groaning roar that shook the very hills and was shattering to endure. If it had occurred in the everyday world, it would have been heard for a hundred miles. Yet no other human heard that sound.

To this day, it haunts some of my waking dreams.

Of course the vision passed. Night faded. The sun rose in a blaze of healing fire. From that altitude, I could see almost the whole of the western Highlands of Scotland, marching north to south, peak after riotous peak, swimming in the golden light of a summer's dawn. If I live to be five hundred years old, I don't expect to have another experience in which the coming of a new day brought such a fabulous wealth of colors, shapes and vivid light. The emotions were keyed up to match; the escape from fear brought me into the realm of such delight that exhilaration and ecstasy are poor and inadequate words.

It was unquestionably the experience of a lifetime and fully justified the hours of cold and misery. Moreover, something of the shaman had awoke within me, I knew.

As the sun climbed higher, the wondrous beauty of those first few minutes faded into the full light of day. The moment had passed for ever. I had been lucky and felt very humble. After that, breakfast, though only a few morsels heated on a solid fuel stove and a welcome cup of hot tea, surpassed the finest meal at the Savoy. In the bright shimmering morning, food never tasted so good.

Maybe it was only relative but the sun was beginning to feel warm by the time I started my descent. I elected for the route south, past the Inaccessible Pinnacle and the great block of *An Stac*. A wild scree run dropped me hundreds of feet quickly, into the shadows of a deep corrie. From there it was all rough moorland grass and rock, down to sea level.

My tired legs soon turned to uncontrollable rubber and I was stumbling frequently by the time I reached my car, parked on the shore. I reported safely to the warden. After that it was a short drive to a hot bath, a second breakfast and a well-earned sleep.

3. Journeys in Another Dimension

I do not know why I was chosen by the Old People, if indeed I was. Perhaps it was connected with the fact that I had been researching into shamanism. As a doctor interested in alternative treatment methods I had decided to learn more about this fascinating mode of healing. It became quickly clear it was far more than just a healing system. It was a kind of ritualized magic on its own terms.

My first glimmering of awareness of alternative realities came from reading US anthropologist Michael Harner's book *The Way Of The Shaman*. In it he describes taking the mind-altering drug *ayahuasca* and going on a dream journey to another world where he met nasty creatures calling themselves the "Masters of the Universe". When he described his experience to a tribal elder, the old sage laughed and said, "That bunch! They always call themselves that. Pay no attention to them. They are only the Masters of the Outer Darkness."

The shock to Harner, the scientist, was the absolute realization that the place he had visited in his dream was quite real but in another dimension. It was not a fantasy or hallucination; the old man, and others, had been there too! From then on Harner made up his mind to study shamanism as a serious scientific topic and established the Foundation for Shamanic Studies. His words had encouraged me to adopt a similarly enquiring, non-dismissive, attitude.

One of the key precepts Harner had found in aboriginal societies all round the world was that of soul retrieval. The shamanic view of sickness is that a part of the individual's soul has become split off and wandered away into alternative space. Given this model, the cure was obvious: the shaman would travel into this other reality (often at great personal risk) and bring back the lost soul part. The feathers, the face paint and the drum beats are all irrelevant, apart from creating the appropriate frame of mind.

It is fashionable, thanks to Hollywood, to laugh at this supposedly primitive medicine and we have the derisory term "witch doctor". But as a practising physician I can share with you my suspicion, which is that more people are healed, world-wide, by this sort of medicine than are helped by antibiotics and other pharmaceuticals. At least it addresses the problem ignored by Western medicine, which is that a person gets sick *for a reason*. The reason is not microbes or cancer cells. Merely killing microbes or cutting away diseased tissue leaves the real sickness unresolved.

The shaman will approach a sick individual as someone who is un-whole. Something is missing, typically a part of the person's soul. When that missing piece is retrieved from wherever in the universe it is hiding and restored to the individual, he or she gets well.

The path to becoming a competent shaman is usually hard and testing, even terrifying.

I read of one Siberian tribe which would select a possible shaman and then push him under the ice on a frozen river. He had to make it over to a second hole in the ice, a few hundreds yards away. If he did, he was acknowledged as a true shaman. If he didn't make it, well then he was a "dud" and I don't suppose many people mourned him.

In another case an Inuit (eskimo) shaman was walled up in an ice house for thirty days without food. Not surprisingly, before the end he was starting to hallucinate, which is often the point of some of these rituals. What was really surprising however is what he saw: a beautiful white blonde woman, something he had never seen in what we are pleased to call "real life".

Let me stress these visions are not shamanism. To me the operative definition of shamanic power is this: *some event or transposition in alternative reality which creates a significant change in this reality.* If all that takes place is altered perception in the shaman's head, critics rightly could argue that it is no more significant than hallucination. But if something happens in our ordinary reality, as a result, then power has been exerted. It matters not whether you call it magic.

For example, a prenatal x-ray showed a foetus with an occluded oesophagus; when born it would not be able to swallow food and would quickly die; operative intervention is not always successful. In this case (true story) the shaman visited the foetus in the womb and rejoined the oesophagus. One week later x-rays are normal and the child is born with no problem. Such an intervention fits my definition of shamanism.

I have no truck with the scientific community who says this cannot happen. Science today is merely a series of dogmas, stagnating more and more, as entrenched opinion refuses to even sanction research into new ideas and derides any line of thought which threatens the status quo. The reason is, of course, that science is no longer the domain of the adventurous thinker but is controlled by big business, which cares more for its investors than the truth, and is headed by salaried professors who have to pay their mortgage: damn the new dawn.

The history of science is ablaze with contradictions and overthrow. There is not a major scientific theory in the last five hundred years that has not been proved wrong – eventually.

In the late nineteenth century, British physicist William Thompson, later the First Baron Kelvin (Lord Kelvin) made a solemn pronouncement that all the main discoveries of science were in place; that it now only needed fine-tuning in the details and where to put the decimal places.

What extraordinary arrogance from so great a man!

Within thirty years, everything he had taught was overthrown by three giant new theories he could never even have dreamed of:

- radio-activity showed that substances could decay and transmute, one to another, exactly as the ancient alchemists had believed
- quantum physics, which revealed a world more strange and beyond imagining than even the fantasies of Lewis Carroll writing "Alice and Wonderland"
- and last but not least Einstein's bizarre theory of Relativity, which simply took away the ground from beneath us, in terms of comprehensible reality

The worlds of Aristotle and Newton had died in three great convulsions.

And why?

Simply because there was another reality out there, waiting to be discovered but was, at that time, unknown... Well, isn't that what other realities are: just other worlds and dimensions that have not yet been discovered? What extraordinary foolishness to say, as modern scientists do, that there are no new places to be discovered! How can they know?

The relentless forces of change and discovery are still at work. In 1957 Hugh Everett, a physicist at Princeton, proposed the idea of infinite universes, each one an alternative variation of reality: what would the world have been like without Hitler? Well, there is a world where Hitler never appeared! What if Jesus had not been crucified or Mohammed not born? What would your life have been like if just one element was different: you did marry that guy or didn't marry that guy?

According to Everett all these universes actually exist. Bryce Seligman popularized and renamed this theory "many-worlds". It's either frightening or inspiring, according to the disposition of your consciousness. These worlds may or may not be accessible to us (we'll see, in time).

Many-worlds certainly gives us magic. It means, in effect, that anything and everything imaginable must have taken place somewhere, some time, in one or other of these universes. There are an infinite number of them, so the possibilities are infinite and cannot be constrained by normal human experience.

Yet the present custodians of knowledge cling to their narrow view as if it were inviolate and could never be challenged. They forget it was once "scientific" to say the earth was flat, that heavier-than-air machines would never fly (Lord Kelvin actually said that, too!) and the atom could not be split into smaller particles.

One hundred and fifty years ago it would have been dismissed as fantasy magic, to send the sound of the human voice round the world, never mind images of the speaker.

I remember this and laugh when shamanism is dismissed as "unscientific". The absolute reality was not, of course, that radio waves were impossible; it was that science did not have an explanation, no model as we say. This has somehow been twisted from "no model" to "what you describe simply could not happen". The reader would do well to think of this example when considering the possibility of magical flying, as described in this text.

Shamanism has failures, of course it does. Like lawyers, doctors, musicians and artists, there are good and bad shamans. For some, the ritual has taken over and become a substitute for the kind of action I am describing. But there are many stories for the inquisitive reader of apparently magical successes by competent shamans so that the results cannot be dismissed over and over as mere delusion or "coincidence", that last intellectual bolt-hole of the pseudo-scientific dunderhead.

To conclude, I would like to introduce one final aspect of the shamanic model. All societies describe another deeper reality than this one: dark, mysterious and shadowy, a sort of metaphorical under-belly of existence. It is probably the origin of the idea of Hades or Hell. In Europe we call it Lower World. It is safer to travel it in the company of your protective "power animal". I have been down the tunnel to Lower World and know with personal certainty it exists. I have met many strange beings there, one of the least challenging of which was a knight calling himself Sir Thomas. He suggested a cure for one of my patients, which worked dramatically! I have never seen him since to thank him.

I introduce the Lower World to the reader only because, for my journeys down there, I had chosen an entry point on Skye, a portal I had discovered years before while wandering the moors. I had no doubt it was a fairy gateway. They were said to glow in the dark and lure unsuspecting travellers, though the one I found was long dead and without apparent energies.

Maybe this presumptuous action of mine had disturbed the interface between realities and somehow opened a connection between me and the Old People of the island, waiting to activate when I appeared again in person…

4. Contact

It was one of those long, lazy July days, so magical in the Hebrides. I had climbed to the peak of a little-known promontory at the north west of Skye, well-named the "air peak" (*Biod an Athair*). As the ground fell away at my feet, I found myself sitting on the edge of a breathtaking cliff, over one thousand feet above the waves below, so distant their sound barely ascended to my eagle's perch. Across the marbled island sea known as the Minch, I could see Lewis, Harris, Benbecula, Eriskay, and the whole chain of outer islands, every one a song in the warm afternoon air. With but little exercise of imagination, one could tug aside the curtain of time and easily see the chieftains' galleys of old, plying across the ancient waters, often bent on murder or revenge.

It was a scene of uttermost serenity, where earth, sky and sea fused in a blue haze of aching beauty.

I noticed the figure about half a mile off, walking along the ridge towards me. He was not wearing a cagoul or boots but seemed to be wrapped in some kind of cloak. I presumed he was a local man and knew the locality well enough to be able to spurn outdoor gear. He carried a stick but seemed nimble and not at all bent.

Suddenly my skin began to bristle with that electric tingle, which is akin to fear, but not quite so negative.

I tried to dismiss the feeling. Perhaps the wind had turned a little chilly; the weather changes so quickly in the far north. I returned my gaze to the scene that had been ravishing my eyes for over an hour.

After what seemed just a few seconds, I can only suppose it must have been longer, I turned with a start to find him standing right next to me. He had covered the intervening few hundred yards unnervingly fast. Again I got the prickling feeling and stood up to confront the stranger. I could see now that he was tall, with greying red hair and shaggy beard, his face wrinkled but kindly and non-confrontational. His eyes were piercing blue and looked patiently into mine as I took a few moments to size him up.

"Beautiful, isn't it?" he said, indicating the panorama. I suppose it was as good a way of saying hello as any.

I nodded in agreement.

"They say if you look far to the west, beyond those islands, you can see…"

"St. Kilda. Yes, I've seen it."

He laughed softly. "I was going to say *Tir nan Og*."

"Ah, the Land of the Ever-Young; the place of ineffable bliss."

"I see we have a Gaelic scholar, though your accent is clearly English." His voice was soft with a musical lilt, like that of the islanders. The language of the Gael is so close to music that when he talks he sings.

"I read a lot. I'm handy with place names."

"So little is written in English about this land and its people, the real people."

"I read a great deal by an author called Seton Gordon."

"My friend Seton, who lives… who lived at Kilmuir in the Trotternish yonder."

"You knew him?"

"Yes, indeed. I met him.. hmmm," he paused, "Many times."

"He wrote a great deal about the clan people, the wildlife and, of course, the fairy folk."

"You first read his book, at school, during a detention. Isn't that correct, Doctor?"

"Why yes, but how did you know…?" Even before I had finished voicing the question, I knew the answer. "You're one of the…" I hesitated, unable to give voice to my thoughts, in a foolish anxiety that I might be mistaken.

"Yes, I am one of the Old People," he said, smiling gently.

"You were playing with me just then," I accused him, smarting from the slight.

"Not really. But when you feel you know someone so well it's hard not to let a revealing remark slip through."

Even though his voice was soft and reassuring, to hear these declarations in such matter-of-fact tones was utterly shocking. My sympathetic nervous system went into overdrive, flooding my blood with adrenalin, causing every nerve to stand on end, my heart raced and I must have gone white as a sheet.

"Steady there," he murmured and caught hold of me. "This is no place to feel dizzy and lose your balance."

"I suppose not," I gasped.

His touch was warm and soft and definitely physical. Well, that was one confusion cleared up. I had heard old stories of mortals having children with fairies. I had always dismissed the idea as nonsense; how could there be procreation between mortal physical matter and something insubstantial?

This fairy was solid enough.

Then I realized, substantial or not, this being had flown several hundred yards along the cliff top. An idea so daring and outrageous leapt into my mind, that I tried to dismiss it. But it wouldn't go away.

"I hope you don't consider this rude or ridiculous but, I mean…."

"Speak your mind, Doctor. I believed there was some moment hanging on this encounter. But if you cannot speak your mind, maybe I was wrong."

"OK. Could you teach me to fly? Flying without wings, I mean; magical flying?"

There, it slipped out. I felt pretty foolish but it *was* the question I would most want to ask a fairy. Wouldn't you? It had not escaped my notice that this figure, this being, was without wings.

"You don't want much, do you?"

"What did you expect me to say was my greatest desire — a pot of gold on the mantel shelf that fills itself eternally?"

"Many might have chosen that."

"Well to me that would be a stupid choice."

He didn't answer but just smiled wryly.

Suddenly I knew that words were useless instruments. Many things took place in the moments that followed, changes and sensations at many levels. But none of it required speech and indeed there was no language to describe even a fraction of what took place between us.

He broke the silence first. "Nobody has asked me this before."

"You are shocked?"

"No."

"Well then?"

"I could teach you *about* flying."

"No, I mean really flying. Or let's not call it flying. Let's just say lifting my body from the ground and having it drift around at will. Could I do it? Can any human learn to do it?"

"Not just any human, no. To learn to fly would require knowledge and power that human beings do not possess."

"To me, that is the whole point. Are you saying a human being could never acquire such knowledge?"

"The human, no. The being, yes."

"Well, then?"

"Flying, Doctor, is not just a matter of finding some previously unknown muscle and exercising it. It is about altering your entire conscious Being from that of a physical entity to one of pure consciousness. That is something easily expressed in words but represents a very great leap for the human mind."

"Such as?"

"You would require a whole different entry into the physical domain you call the "real" world, a completely new understanding of such concepts as time, space, creation and viewpoint."

"But if I did have the necessary knowledge and perspective, I would be able to fly magically?"

"Assuredly you could fly. But it would not be magical! You would know the secret. Magic occurs only when the process is unknown. If it is known, it is not magical."

That's logical, I had to admit. Once you knew the conjuror's secret, the illusion lost all air of mystery and surprise.

"I notice you don't have wings."

"Doctor, I'm surprised at you. For fairies, if you must use that term," a tone of disdain appeared in his voice. I would ask him about fairy ego and emotions some time, "With wings is human whimsy, perpetrated by persons who have never met any of the Old People. Wings are needed only to accord with the laws of physics. The kind of flying we are talking about does not require uplift from air pressure. Nothing as heavy as a twelve-stone man is able to fly in this way."

I was chagrined. Of course the heaviest bird weighs less than a human child. Moreover the formidable muscles (chicken and turkey breast) that would be required to beat the wings of a mythical creature of human form would be hard to imagine.

No, it had to be magic.

I observed that he had made a decision of some kind...

"Meet me tomorrow in the Piper's Cave nearby. I will ask you some pertinent questions in turn. Get plenty of sleep."

With that he was gone. Not even a goodbye, I said to myself peevishly.

It only took a moment for the doubts to crowd in, like vultures at a carcass. Of course it had all been an illusion, a dream. I must ask the landlady more about what was in the packed lunch.

Even so, though I was baffled and disconcerted, I felt somehow different. Some door had opened in my mind and even if it had been a bad piece of ham in the sandwiches, it was not going to settle down without fulfilment. We would see tomorrow where all this was going.

I lingered on the peak, watching the sun slowly transform the Minch into a couldron of molten metal. I could not help but think of the much-misunderstood alchemists and their pursuit of the transformation of base metal into gold. Here nature had done it, right before my eyes.

The alchemists too had desired the spiritual powers we would call magic – not as a fast road to riches but as a path to unearthly powers. They were seekers who tried to investigate the natural world but with little or no method and no technology to help them: forerunners of modern scientists but with a mystical bent.

Since the world—as they perceived it—was a mystery, they naturally assumed that its secrets would turn out to be elusive, divine, transformational, even demonic. But to discover those secrets, they supposed, would bring the initiate immense power. Secrets at a far deeper level than ordinary reality.

Perhaps they were right? Now I had suddenly opted to join their ranks. I, a medical doctor, a scientist, was to become an alchemist!

As I walked home I thought of a fellow doctor from long centuries ago, named Jabir (aka. Abu Musa Jabir ibn Hayyan). He was a true mystic or sufi and a prominent Islamic alchemist, pharmacist, philosopher and physician. He was my early brother. Jabir was also a chemist, astronomer and astrologer, engineer, geologist and physicist; a true polymath.

His name was Latinised as "Geber" in the Christian West and in thirteenth century Europe an anonymous writer produced a body of alchemical and metallurgical writings under the pen-name Geber. This person is usually referred to as Pseudo-Geber.

The real Jabir's works were deliberately written in a highly esoteric code, so that only those who had been initiated into his alchemical school could understand them. It is believed the word gibberish originally referred to this man's writings. So he's in our dictionaries! That's how famous he was.

Several technical terms introduced by Jaber, such as alkali, have found their way into various European languages and have become part of our scientific vocabulary.

A crater of the moon is named Geber, to commemorate him.

Unfortunately, Jabir got caught up in the politics of the day; he spent the last twelve years of his life under house arrest. The world was not ready for such a man. What an exemplary spirit he was.

I wonder if he ever tackled the issue of magical flying…

Discussion

Alchemy has now become a vigorous academic field! Well, not the pursuit of transmutation and immortality. But the history of alchemy is now studied deeply, for its diverse and exceptionally fascinating insights.

One can even ascribe to it the beginnings of scientific enquiry and the method of testing which we so prize as a measure of rationality today.

They say the word alchemy probably derives from the old French alkemie; from the Arabic al-kimia: "the art of transformation." Some scholars believe the Arabs borrowed the word *kimia* from Greek for transmutation. Remember almost all our mathematical and scientific knowledge came from the Arabs, they having got it first from the Greeks.

It's a schoolroom myth that we inherited our modern civilized knowledge from the Ancient Greeks. All that connection went up in smoke with the great library of Alexandria. In truth, our Western civilization and its intellectual prowess is built on that of the Middle East, not early Europe.

I always regarded alchemy as one of the weirdest of all subjects. I could never understand, when I was a kid, how grown men could seriously believe in the idea of changing base metals into gold. Or that the Philosopher's Stone could make them immortal. So I looked down on alchemists, as most true-blue scientists still do today. They were fools, given to humbug.

But my perceptions have totally changed, since I grew up and learned more. I think others are beginning to see them in a different light too.

In fact the alchemists were the great visionaries of ancient and Medieval times. They were trying to escape from everyday reality. They were convinced that somewhere, just beyond the curtain of experience, lay a vast and magical world of phantasms and wonder. They pursued the goal of gaining entry into this mystical kingdom with a purpose and intensity that made them seem like men apart.

Several early alchemists, such as Zosimos of Panopolis, were aware of this spiritual aspect of alchemy and proclaimed it in their writings. Organic and inorganic chemical substances, physical states, and molecular material processes were mere metaphors for spiritual entities, spiritual states and ultimately, spiritual transformations.

Thus, both the transmutation of common metals into gold and the universal panacea symbolized evolution from an imperfect, diseased, corruptible and ephemeral state towards a perfect, healthy, incorruptible and everlasting state; and the philosopher's stone then represented some mystic key that would make this evolution possible.

We could now liken alchemists to quantum physicists, who also have stood tiptoe on the very threshold of another world entirely, one separated from the reality of everyday existence.

It gave me a swell of exhilaration that I should now be among these men of yore. The ability to fly without wings seemed no less magical and unreal than the ability to change lead into gold or find the key to immortality.

Suddenly, the whole history of intellect, science and philosophy flowed before me as a living river…

And I leapt in!

5. I Pass The Test

I wasn't sure I would ever see the Old One again. But he was there, waiting for me on the shore. He had a small wizened staff of hazel.

The Piper's Cave was close by the old McCrimmon school of piping at Borreraig, beyond Dunvegan. Legend has it the music masters sat in there for hours at a stretch, alone with their thoughts, and composed the old classical music of the pipes, haunting pentatonic melodies of great power and beauty, written at a time when the rest of Europe was still struggling to shake off its mediaeval musical limitations. The slow rhythmic beating of the sea was undoubtedly a factor in their many compositions. This very cave was said to be where the great master composed his glorious tune *Maol Donn* or McCrimmon's Sweetheart. I can play it myself, on a good day and with a tail wind!

The shelter was indeed fortunate, since it turned out to be one of those wetter than wet days for which Skye is famous. Not for nothing it is called the "misty isle". Arguably, we were also less likely to be interrupted though, as it happened, a family did progress down to the shore while we were there. A small boy entered the cave and looked around with curiosity. For a moment he seemed to stare straight at us and then ran off as his mother called. It was as if the child had seen nothing but a vague dark shadow, with no forms.

His first question floored me. "Why would you like to learn to fly?"

I had not expected this as an opener. It was probably the hardest question of all. I certainly had no ready answer.

"I don't exactly know," I started off, "It would feel amazing and powerful and invincible."

"But these are just reasons of self-aggrandizement. Not very worthy motives, if you don't mind me saying. If I were to teach you anything about flying, you would have to persuade me better than that. What other reasons can you give?"

I hesitated.

"Speak!" he demanded, "Don't wait for the intellectual dross to surface." He banged his stick on the ground.

"What I mean is that I want to learn something new, something that science cannot yet answer, something magical and wonderful from another place."

"That's just veneer; surface flim flam. What is the real reason? Answer!" He banged down his stick again. Now he sounded like one of the Zen Masters of old. *"If you call it a stick, you trick yourself into accepting restricting labels. If you say it is not a stick, you lie! Speak!"* demanded Shuzen. Pupil after pupil could not answer and was subjected to a painful whack with the stick. Until one student grabbed it from the Master and snapped it in half. *"Good!"* beamed Shuzen. *"You're learning fast!"*

There are many accounts of the stick being broken over the pupil's head, as the exasperated Master tried to get his point across.

I tried not to flinch.

"I want to cross over that boundary between magical and merely human. I want to transcend the here-and-now, connect with God and the angels and all past places in history."

"That's better. Now, what other reasons can you offer? Speak! Quickly." Bang bang bang went the stick.

"It seems to me that flying is among the highest spiritual accomplishments a soul can attain to."

"Explain!" His eyes flashed but this time the stick arm remained still.

I told him about the shamanic journeys and how I viewed these in terms of human spiritual development. "Yet how much more there is to learn about one's self, in order to conquer..."

I slowed down again.

"Yes, yes? To conquer..." He was excited and eager for me to reveal my deepest thoughts.

"To conquer unknownness about one's soul, to learn the workings of reality, to attain..."

"Yes?"

"To attain a full and compelling grasp of the truth. One could not fly by walking the path of lies and pretense – only by arriving at the ultimate truth, the deepest order of the Cosmos, the final secret of Being."

"Pass!"

"Pass?"

"You've passed the test. I will show you how to fly."

I don't know if I was more excited by apprehension or by anticipation.

"What is it going to take?"

"Doctor, it will require nothing less than a total revolution of your connections with the Cosmos. Like all humans, you seem to have lost touch with your native state of consciousness. It is that higher fully conscious self that holds the power you need to tap into."

"But we are fully conscious, though I admit there is much experience of life hidden in the subconscious."

"Trust me, you do not know of the *fully conscious* self, it is far above and beyond the mind."

"You sound like Gurdjieff. He said *the biggest barrier to consciousness is the belief that we are already conscious.* His view of human life was that we were mainly automatic machines, answering patterns and habits, rather than real aware thinking entities."

"He was far from wrong."

"Well that doesn't apply to some of us, who have worked hard on opening up our eyes and ears to other, deeper worlds."

"That is so. And if I may say, is the reason I am here talking to you at all."

I was more baffled than flattered.

For The Reader:

Try some of Gurdieff's writings, if you've a mind. Peter Ouspensky is a good starting point; critics say he got it wrong but he knew Gurdieff and, I think, translates him very well.

You can also look at the profound and heretical works of Madame Blavatsky and consider this: could any part of what she said be true? How would that change the world you live in, if she had uncovered a kind of "physics of the soul", as opposed the everyday physics?

6. Out-Of-Body, Out Of Mind

Next morning, after breakfast, I went to the car, intending to retrace the first day's steps. He was waiting outside. I realized he would probably show up, whatever I was doing, and ceased to worry about arrangements to meet.

"Let's go for a walk," he said.

I looked around, wondering if anyone else could see this fairy. But no other human being was to be seen. "You've all missed your chance!" I thought to myself smugly. I immediately regretted this unkind and conceited thought. I was acutely embarrassed by the realization that the fairy might very well be able to know what I was thinking.

We set out towards the shore. As we walked, I noticed that once again people seemed not to see us. I greeted one woman, cutting peats for the winter fire, but she acted as if she did not hear me. It had happened in the cave. Perhaps in his presence I too was invisible to normal people.

"I'd like to ask about out-of-body experiences. It seems to me there are some crucial similarities to flying."

"Please define your term out-of-body experience."

"Well, leaving the body in the mind's eye, drifting up and floating off. Your view point is not that of the eyes of the body but from the self viewpoint, higher up, as if flying. In fact, characteristically, the body is seen at a distance, though some goons have been heard to say "I'm over there", which of course means they are not out of their body at all."

"Have you been out of your body in this awareness mode, Doctor?"

"Yes, many times. It started when I was in my teens, learning to meditate. As a physician I became aware that it often happens to people who are stressed, exhausted or mentally very low. But I long to be able to do it at will and for long periods; outside with full perception, that is. This phenomenon is now discussed openly, whereas in the sixties decade when I first encountered it, people scoffed and nobody would readily admit to such a thing."

"And how is that different from the process humans call 'astral travel'?"

"Basically astral travel is an earlier term applied to the same thing. Maybe just a metaphor. But the picture is blurred by talk of astral bodies, a phantom body that walked for you in the other dimension."

"That's not the same thing. You don't need astral bodies or ectoplasm cords, or anything of the sort; these are for the weak and uncertain, not for the true flier." He sounded quite pedantic about this.

"I remember the professor of psychiatry talking pompously about people 'imagining' that they were drifting out of their bodies and asked his pupils: was this definable madness or just imagination? I dared to suggest that maybe they really were de-coupling from their bodies and seeing from outside. The mediocrity of intellect demonstrated by his reply enabled me to realize he had nothing whatever to teach me about the mind, and I never went back to his tutorials."

"Medical people seem sadly unaware of the importance of consciousness in the process of healing or indeed in the initiation of the sickness process."

"The fact remains, out-of-body always seems to be out of conscious control of the individual who experiences it. Then a few years ago, a man called Robert Monroe developed a means of getting people out the body, to travel in what he called the Second State."

"Shouldn't that be First State?"

"I now think so. Anyway, he achieved it by playing different electronic frequencies to different sides of the brain, a technique we call hemi-sync."

"I know of this work. Our people have sometimes met his travelers, voyaging in the Other World."

"Would this method help in learning to fly?"

"Not as such. But it would bring about a better understanding that conscious awareness is not a function of the brain."

"Well that brings me to an important question: why then is it that people who have strange psychic and other experiences, levitation, seeing visions and so on, are often in a state of extreme brain distress, such as hunger or sleep deprivation? Doesn't that suggest that the brain is involved?"

"That is one explanation that might suggest itself. But the real reason is that when these mental deprivation states occur, it means that the physical is allowed to intrude *less* in the process of awareness. Say rather that access to states of higher awareness is what happens when the brain is kept out of the picture, to a degree, by its malfunction."

"I suppose that is the nature of a spiritual fast: after a sufficient state of brain starvation is reached, it begins to shut down and the spiritual voice can be heard?"

"I like that explanation."

"Well, how do drugs work?"

"Drugs?"

"LSD and other junk of that sort is supposed to do it. People undergoing an anaesthetic prior to an operation sometimes get this manifestation and can be very frightened by it."

"Once again, the supernatural, as you sometimes call it, will surface once the physiological is disabled. But my view is that drugs are unlikely to turn a dull, leaden awareness into a vibrant spiritual being."

"Which is what only a cabbage-head would hope!"

"But it could just cut loose a being who is ready to make the jump. Unfortunately, there is always a come-down afterwards. When these artificial means are used, it is always frustrating and disappointing to the individual, to be unable to continue the sublime experiences without further use of the drug. And of course what happens is that, through time, the drug has less and less effect. Higher and higher doses, or experiments with newer substances, fail to recapture the transcendental moments once freely experienced. Does that alone not tell you that brain chemistry is not the origin of the divine experience? Those deluded individuals who follow this path do not see that they are allowing the physical to conquer more and more of the soul? That is not liberation but psychic slavery."

"It has been pitiful to me to see the state of a brilliant mind, such as John C. Lilly, so damaged by repeated exposure to chemicals."

"It is a pity that this Mr Lilly could not understand fully what the dolphins were trying to tell him. He would have been better to speak with the Old People, who could share his own language more acutely."

"What I see is that these out-of-body experiences are like flying but do not require such enormous spiritual power. Is that not correct?"

"They are of an order of magnitude to flying, as atomic power is to coal and steam."

"Well, as I have learned so far, there appear to be three states: flying without a body, flying with a body, which demands so much more. But then there is the highest state of all, not needing a body. Not being incarnated?"

"That would seem to cover it."

"So if one transcends all material connections, one would be an Ascended Master and not return to this conjoint physical world?"

"Probably not."

"Are you an Ascended Master?"

It was obvious I was going to ask. You would too. He smiled and paused, carefully considering his reply.

"No. That is a quaint term that humans use for someone they admire. An Ascended Master, in my view, remains very connected to Earth and those to whom he manifests. To ascend, as you call it, would be to retire from the field of action."

"So this is like show business, you mean—divine souls hanging out here on Earth and these lower planes because they enjoy the acclaim?"

"Your language, Doctor, a trifle excessive."

"But Buddha – you know Lord Buddha?"

"Son, we don't exactly read the newspapers in my world—but yes, I know Lord Buddha."

"Have you met him?"

"You mean the energy being that manifested as Buddha?"

"Yes, I suppose that is what I mean."

There was hardly time to reflect that my former tutors and professors would think me certifiably insane to be having this kind of conversation with an entity which did not, in fact, exist!

"I am that energy," he said, simply and unceremoniously.

"Really? Wow! I mean…" His reply had almost taken my breath away. Could I be talking to Buddha? What did such a concept really mean?

"We all are divine energy. You are. It is the divine essence in all of us. Perhaps the greatest incarnation of it was in Gotama Siddartha but the point he tried to make was that his sweet energy is everywhere, abundant and available to anyone who claims it."

"And flying will help me to find it?"

"Of that there can be no doubt. Also *vice versa*, finding that divine energy will help you fly. The quest is one and the same. Come tomorrow and we will talk again."

His voice held the clear emphasis that there would be no more that day. Nevertheless, I was exulted. Could it be that by the time the sun had set next day I would have learned to fly and become a magical being! My heart surged with excitement.

Alone with my thoughts, I once more walked along the sea's edge, listening to the musical rock and woosh of the waves. There is something in the sea, the ocean, some energy or rhythm that is so profound for humans that I cannot hear the sound without being transported into profound mind spaces.

Truly the Celt was aware of *Ceol na Mara*, the haunting Music Of The Sea.

For the reader:

I have learned a number of things about OBEs over the years. It happens a lot but most people don't recognize it, on the principle that such a thing can't happen, therefore it doesn't!

Thanks to the principles outlined in this book, I have been aware for decades that I am living outside my body. When I close my eyes for sleep at night, I am outside. I feel bigger than my body-self. It is a sense of stepping outdoors, into a garden of greater Being. When I open my eyes again, I revert to the smaller "self". Surely this is indicating that the "real" world is limited and limiting?

Try this exercise, to test your perception of self, body and exterior perception: sitting in a chair relaxing or in bed but not too sleepy, close your eyes and start to feel for the edges of your Being. Go outwards and it should be easy to recognize that you are far vaster than the boundaries of your skin. Indeed, if it goes well for you, after a few sessions, I am sure you will quickly realize that your Being is infinite. It is as big as the universe you can "sense".

When you have been successful at this, imagine yourself drifting up out of your body and away to some favourite place. Circle around and look at things from different angles, and from above, a view point we do not normally occupy. Be alert for any surprise perceptions. Soon you may suspect that you are not dreaming or inventing the sensations!

7. The Three Universes

The following day was something of a disappointment. Instead of flying I was treated to another philosophy lesson. It was difficult to tell, in these early sessions, where it was all leading.

"You must learn, Doctor, of the division of reality into three clear and distinct universes."

"That's ridiculous. Even if there are three – or three hundred – we can only occupy one universe at a time, surely?"

"You must listen and not argue, if we are to make progress."

"Sorry." But I'm right, I thought to myself arrogantly. A universe means everything, only-one, that's the meaning of the word, uni- is all or one. Then again, I was unsettled by remembering the possibility he could read my thoughts. Better behave!

"The first, and in many ways the most important, universe is your own personal universe. It is found within and it obeys only those laws of reality you choose. In it the laws of physics may be suspended and consequently time and space can take on whatever mode you decide. You could have negative gravity, houses that float in the air, and humans with wings, like angels."

"That's just what we call imagination or dreams, nothing more."

"Nevertheless, it is your own domain and has all the properties and inducements of a universe. It has space, time, matter and energy. Think about this."

I did and I could see he was right, in a way.

"The second universe is that of other people. The reality they hold may not be the same interpretation of existence as your own."

"But there is the real universe to settle disputes about what exists and what doesn't."

"That brings me to the third universe, which is *agreed upon reality*. The world of matter, energy, space and time. It is important to understand that this universe does not have absolute control of what is real. It is only what is agreed by the perception of all conscious entities which subscribe to it."

"This still remains the senior universe, though I readily admit there can be personal experiences at variance with time and space."

"No son, I will have you know that this agreed reality is the one blinding illusion that every human being is slave to. The so-called real world is a shocking fake, as the one you call Buddha tried to teach thousands of years ago. It doesn't even exist, except that you choose to perceive that it does."

"That's sounds like Bishop George Berkeley, one of the British Empiricists..."

"Shut up for once. You are here because there are things you don't know."

I began to see that intellectual knowledge, learning you might call it, was a definite barrier to what he was driving at.

"I just don't see how the personal universe can be senior to actual reality."

"I repeat, the physical universe is not real. Even if it were, you can only inter-relate with your perception of it. In the end it is only what you perceive to exist that is true."

"What's true for me is the truth?"

"Exactly."

"But perception is the weakest road there is to truth. It is so easy to fool the senses. People see or imagine things all the time that even they, at a later time, realize did not in fact exist. Modern consciousness psychologists are stuck on this point. I do not believe they are studying consciousness; just perception."

"Well then, it is but a short step to the truth that you may perceive whatever you personally perceive and that is your universe, no more, no less. You cannot prove the physical universe is this way or that way, because everybody else is in the same difficult position regarding perception."

I began to see the relevance of this. But I was suspicious.

"Are you saying that if I believe I'm flying and that's what I perceive, then even if everyone else sees me stuck on the ground, that the "truth" is that I'm flying?"

"No. Those are your words. But I am saying that the physical universe accords with what is perceived. It is not the other way round, no matter what so-called scientists try to tell you."

"Well, I do know that certain physicists, the quantum people particularly, have realized that there is no objective universe, without the presence of human consciousness."

"Then we may take this as our first working hypothesis in regard to flying."

"So I must fly in my own universe before I can fly in the real world?"

"A very good place to begin."

"I don't want this to be just in my mind," I protested. "I want this to be real."

"What part of your mind is not touching something real?" he asked.

Ah, a clever question!

"Well, the thoughts and dreams part."

"So you admit there is a reality beyond the confines of the physical universe?"

"Yes, I suppose so," I replied, sensing a trap.

"In what sense is it a universe then, meaning it encompasses everything?"

I was flummoxed. He was right, of course. If the universe means "all one", then nothing can lie outside it. But I knew right away he meant there truly are things that are not part of anything. There are things from "Beyond"; *mas alla*, as the Spanish say!

"Ah, but what about multiple universes. Is there such a thing? You, I suppose, would know."

"Explain this idea."

"You know, Hugh Everett, the guy from Harvard, 1957? Everett argued that reality is a quantum thing. We know that every possible alternative has a suspended state called a wave function. Only when the function collapses does it go one way or the other and as a result we get what we call reality. But supposing the wave function doesn't collapse but both realities continue to exist? That means the whole universe divides in two at that point, one universe where it did happen and one universe where it didn't happen, running in parallel. Later, this formulation was popularized and renamed many-worlds by Bryce Seligman DeWitt in the nineteen sixties and seventies. Many worlds views reality as a multi-branched tree, in which every infinite possible outcome is realized, somewhere..."

"Yes, yes," he interrupted impatiently," I know this interpretation, Doctor. But what relevance does it have and how do you suppose it will help us with the matter in hand?"

"Well," I smiled—just for once I'd got one over on him here... "If there are an infinite number of universes out there, with an infinite number of possibilities..."

"Yes?"

"And an infinite number of possible versions of me, or doppelgangers, doing everything that can be described or imagined... That includes a double of me somewhere out there who is able to fly by magic and is doing so, even as we speak!"

I looked at him expecting a compliment. My argument, I knew, was irrefutable. Infinite possibilities means what it says: everything, anything, an infinite number of variations. There must be universe somewhere in which I could already fly…

He gave not a flicker of a smile or expression.

"Come now," he snapped. "We are wasting time on this intellectual repartee."

He had me close my eyes and visualize my body floating above the ground. When I had assured him I could do this, he then had me transport it from place to place. That wasn't too difficult. But when he said imagine a group of people watching and expressing disbelief, I could no longer picture myself flying. I was rooted to the ground, even in my own universe. This was most interesting.

He seemed to have proved his point, with a cunning trick.

"You see, you accord so little respect for your own view, Doctor, and that is tragic and comic at the same time. Why must you only believe what other people allow you to believe?"

"This is what we have always been taught, since childhood."

"This teaching marks the end of childhood and the onset of adult cynicism. Notice I refer to a child-like view, not child-*ish*, which is unflattering. This is most pertinent to your quest, Doctor, since every child knows that flying is easy. Peter Pan, dragons, fairies, witches and wizards all do it."

"But isn't that the same as agreement but in another guise?"

"You are correct. The lesson here is that you may agree with anything you so choose and then abandon the agreement, whenever it suits you."

"But this is very difficult. It may take an enormous effort of will to overthrow lifelong beliefs."

"Not will, Doctor, but knowledge. It is no secret that the only human fliers, apart from an occasional ripple in long-established reality, are those wise beings who have taken the trouble to learn the secrets of the Higher Reality. It requires an especially clean and uncluttered view of things to be able to perceive the differences in the world of self, others and as a property of the physical universe."

"Yet I must?"

"I assure you, it is essential."

Phew!

For the reader:

Sit down and relax in a quiet space, where you will not be disturbed. Breathe gently to calm your thoughts and then, in your mind's eye, see yourself flying as I have described. Have your body move around. Control it!

If the spectre of yourself flying, or levitating as some people call it, does not excite you at this stage, the quest may not be for you. But you may still benefit from the numerous mind-expanding revelations of the fairy.

8. Dream time

Once back in Manchester and at work in the Emergency Room in the hospital, the dreams began. They were mild at first but gradually grew more and more intense as the project continued. I dream very little normally. Science tells us, of course, that we all dream a little every night but most of them vanish on waking. What electro-encephalograms cannot tell us is why, sometimes, we wake with vivid recollections of what we have been dreaming.

There is a whole industry geared to interpreting dreams and there are many self-styled experts in this most delusory of all fields of knowledge. True, there are themes which make sense. For many years after my wife left I continued to dream of a broken down, empty and ruined house on a lonely rock out to sea. Huge, terrifying waves swirled on all sides and threatened to sweep me away, as I clung helplessly to the shattered walls. It would not take a genius to see this represented a broken home, unable to nurture and protect the family from the onslaught of life's turbulent forces.

But what of dreaming about giving water to drink from a teaspoon to three large lobsters (true case): what could that possibly mean? Answers please on a postcard… as the BBC used to say.

Most dreams, it is understood, are ways in which to deal with the issues encountered during the ordinary reality of the day. Events are run through once more, often in bizarre format, perhaps trivialized and thus made into something comfortable which can be filed away in memory. A cat may become a tiger in dream time; emotional clouds turn to tumbling feathers, which makes light of the pain; running while being chased and being unable to get away can represent events which are not being faced up to. The more vivid the dream, it is generally held, the more serious and consuming the matters of the day to which they refer.

That, at least, is the present state of knowledge.

But I quickly began to suspect otherwise. Whether the fairy's words had triggered something deep within my psyche, I could not say, but for me the rules of dreaming suddenly did not seem to apply as they should. Oh, I had my share of routine dreaming and those too seemed more vivid than normal. I had one horror vision of flame and smoke in the sky, with distraught souls suddenly cut off from their object of love and devotion, which foreshadowed the infamous attack on the World Trade Center by less than a month; it *could* have been prescient knowledge. But most of the unreality focused on my association with daily events which affected me personally.

Day after day I would dream of strange, but seemingly inconsequential matters; then this material turned up in a real life situation. This was back to front: I was supposed to have the experience first and then dream it away safely into the recesses of my mind and (apparently) forget it. I am not against the idea of pre-cognition – but like everyone else have always thought of it as a rare and special event that happens to rare and gifted individuals, such as Edgar Cayce or the Brahan Seer from Skye.

Then, by chance, I came across J W Dunne's fascinating little book *An Experiment With Time*. Dunne too had had strange, prescient dreams, some quite prophetic on a grand scale. For example, he dreamt of an island exploding, with the loss of four thousand lives. Several days later, he read in the papers an account of the Martinique disaster, in which the volcano erupted, at a loss of *forty* thousand lives (this was in the days before radio or Transatlantic telegraph).

Dunne fell on the explanation that perhaps the data came first, then the dream but that the subject *thought he remembered having the dream the previous night*, a trick of the mind known to medicine as identifying paramnesia. In other words science's explanation is simply "false memory". But Dunne soon came to the same conclusion as myself, which is that too many incidents occurred which made this impossible to accept as the true explanation. Following Dunne's example, I started noting down my dreams in detail: a hard copy account *before* anything in real life had occurred. Sure enough, time and again events occurred which were mirrored by some detail in waking experience.

It was as if I was seeing time, or at least my portion of time, running in reverse, like a car traveling backwards. This, I felt sure, was the reason for the majority of *dèja vu* experiences – not a past life but events had been recently pre-played in the mind and then largely forgotten.

Like everyone else, I still wanted to dismiss the idea of seeing the future as ridiculous. This was made easier by the fact that no forward looking vision ever fully fitted the description of later events in real life. There were tantalizing similarities, sometimes startling correspondences, but nothing which amounted to unequivocal proof that the arrow of time could fly backwards to the drawn bow. Even the dramatic dream which might have foreshadowed the World Trade Center calamity was too vague to be resolved into a flaming building, never mind *which building*.

It was also easier and convenient to dismiss an idea which would turn me into an unwilling freak. Extra Skills: "*Clairvoyance*", wouldn't look too good on my resumé.

But then, says Dunne, came the shocking, indeed outrageous, notion — which is that everyone has the dreaming experience of dipping into the future, it's just that they don't remember it, once back in the waking state. This would make perfect sense; since the mind would tell the dreamer that precognition was "impossible" and therefore the memory would obligingly overlook any instance that showed it might occur. To test this out he recruited several friends and had them all keep detailed records of their dreams, which he later analyzed for content. Now while the experiment did not reveal that sleepers always dream of the future, incidences of correspondence did occur repeatedly which could only be explained by some contact with the future time line.

The scientifically-minded reader may, at this point, bring to mind David Bohm's bizarre but believable theory of the "Holographic Universe". Most people think the important characteristic of a hologram is that images appear in 3-D. But what is far more significant is that every portion of the picture contains the whole image, down to the last detail. Cut a photograph in two and you have two halves of the original image; but cut a hologram in two and you have *two identical complete versions of the image*. Moreover, this can go on to infinity – simply break off a tiny corner of the holographic picture and that still contains the entire image. No matter how many times the image is split, each residual portion contains *everything* that was in the original image – hence the term (w)hologram. Now, says Bohm (incidentally, a gifted and highly respected physicist, far from the lunatic fringe), what if the universe is made in the same way as a hologram: *each and every portion of the universe, no matter how tiny, contains the entire picture of the whole, the totality of past, present and future?*

Bohm's hypothesis is fascinating but I reject it, as usually stated in physical terms, and my personal belief is that the allness-of-everything is in the conscious psyche of our souls, not in the material substance of the universe (as Bohm posits). True, that consciousness may permeate the allness-of-everything, so it practically amounts to the same thing. The difference, however, is crucial. Were the encoded information only to exist in the physical, we would need access to the key or code. If it exists within the conscious glory of all beings, than we only have to reflect inwardly, on the nature of consciousness, on truth and reality, to discover whatsoever we wish. This sounds like the discredited approach of the ancient Greeks: they *thought* about scientific matters but were not big on putting things to the test. With the twentieth century demise of a non-subjective universe, they may have had the right approach after all!

Whatever the mechanism, strange things were happening to me, since contact with Other World. I found it hard to be sure of anything. I began to feel that my life was following the dreams. It made more sense, in view of the three-universes model. Was I staring at proof that consciousness precedes reality and not the other way round? I heard the fairy's words in my head — what we call the real world is a dream, the illusion is reality. But then that begs the question: what are dreams, anyway? Clearly nocturnal visions come in an altered state of consciousness, or supposedly an unconscious state. But maybe this is the real conscious state and that presented by the machinations of the brain during waking hours mere chemical humbug that we have learned to depend on, as if it were our very selves. This would be a huge joke. Like the ostrich sticking its head into the sand in an attempt to blank out reality!

One of the important questions which Dunne took up was: does this time reversal effect only occur in dream time or can it be detected in waking states? If it happens, how could we detect it? Dunne hit upon the idea of selecting a book he had never read and, by concentrating on it, try to get some insight into what was within the covers. By all accounts he had considerable success. Sometimes the words and descriptions were only foreseen vaguely (but still statistically significant) and at other times the choice of words was remarkably correct. Dunne describes one experience of seeing an image of a clock showing 10.30, before reading a detective novel. It turned out that a clock showing exactly 10.30 was crucial to unravelling the entire murder mystery. In at least one instance the description of an object did not appear in the book, even in disguise, but he saw the exact scene on the streets of London some weeks later. This was very weird in my view.

I could not help thinking of Edgar Cayce, the brilliant 20th Century American clairvoyant, who made the outrageous claim that he could put a book under his pillow while sleeping, and know what was in the book next day.

Obviously I wanted to try the prediction experiment with books. The first attempt was an impressive success, until I realized I had read the book before! Next I tried *The Journey of Alvarez Cabral to Brazil and India* (translated by William Brooks Greenlee), which I was absolutely sure I had not read, ever! No words would come but I got a clear mental image picture of a group of strange animals, half man and half chicken, with a most peculiar gait. The text was turgid and boring to read but within two score pages I came across what I was looking for: a description of the customs of the Tupinamba Indians of the Brazil coast. They glued on bird feathers for a ritual dance.

As I continued over several texts there were a number of intriguing correspondences, which together added up to the strong inference that I was somehow making contact with what was inside the covers. Most notable was *Roxana* by Daniel Defoe. Everyone has heard of or read ***Robinson Crusoe***, based on the real life figure of Alexander Selkirk. But I had never even heard of any other of Defoe's works. As soon as I touched the cover of ***Roxana***, I heard five words, clearly and rhythmically, all starting with a p: pwattier, protestant, publican, portion and prostitute.

It took but little time to find these words; Poitier was the French city, the publican turned out to be a brewer and *portion* was an old word for a bride's dowry. I think prostitution would be a strong word to describe what takes place in the remainder of the book but the case for prescience was strongly enhanced by the feverish and naughty goings on!

I was by now convinced that time did not have such a fierce grip over our lives as people supposed. True, Einstein's theory of Relativity makes it clear that what is present time for A can be future time for B but now I began to wonder if past, present and future might not all be present together. I knew vaguely such ideas had been debated but it was another thing altogether to experience it. I knew I was viewing matters from my personal frame of reference in what is customarily called the "present".

There were many aphorisms to the effect that "the present is all we have". But then what was this *present*? Supposedly it was the instant of our conscious attention as it progressed through events, some of which have not yet been experienced and some of which have been. The present was a kind of interface between what had gone before and what would be. This splitting of the time line into past, present and future we call tensed time but some scientific theories of time reject this familiar framework and say it is only an illusion, based on our apparent experience of time.

But even the difficulty of describing this order of events should make one suspicious. For one thing, all descriptions of time need a second time frame from which to describe its passing. But this second time frame needs yet a third time to define it. This goes on into infinity and is the main reason science now rejects the "real" time of the Newtonian universe. Time is, to use Einstein's famous term, "relative".

Since it is, in essence, relative to the viewpoint of the observer, that ought to have alerted everyone to the fact that conscious viewpoint is the source of all reality, exactly as it says in the Hindu ***Vedas***. Unfortunately this collection of brilliant creationist philosophy was written by worthy but non-white races and has therefore been eclipsed in Western thinking.

Where Dunne fails, in my view, is that he never arrives at the real destination, which is that thought, consciousness, is controlling reality and not merely inter-reacting with it passively. Long before I met the fairy again I had gone beyond the suspicion that I was penetrating the future; I had formed the opinion that I was contributing to it, helping create it, in small ways at first but then more and more boldly.

In was an important step to make.

For the reader:

Try the two experiments given by J W Dunne:

1. Record your dream material, night by night. Using a shut off point of no more than one week (Dunne says 2 days for more significance), look for the similarity of material. The hardest part of this task is to accept that there could be any prescient association; your mind will automatically reject any such possibility. You must condition yourself to look at possibilities. Also, Dunne warns, just describe exactly what you saw in the dream, not any interpretation. Two very bright moving discs means just that: do not say "car headlights coming towards me", in case it turns out to be an animal with

reflecting eyes after dark, in which case you would have looked at your notes and not spotted why the prediction failed to appear.

2. Try to look for precognitive material in the waking state. The simplest way to do this is to use books. Obtain books you know you have not read before and think about each for a day or so; sleep on it. Whatever comes into your mind, write it down. Then read the book and see if it appears. I have had phrases from the very first page; Dunne too.

Remember, foresight may not come in the form of words but an image. You may care to add Cayce's input and try the experiment of putting the book under your pillow and, on waking, see what comes to mind and record it, just as you would with a dream. Then read the book!

A complete and satisfying experiment would be to show that you scored much higher with the Cayce technique, proving him correct.

9. Is Space Real?

A month later I returned again to Skye. The weather on this occasion was very different: Atlantic squalls washing in all day, bringing endless grey clouds and rain. I spent most of the day walking at the Northern end of the promontory and was quite hurt when the fairy man did not appear to me.

Next morning I drove to McCleod's Tables, low flat-topped peaks near Dunvegan. According to legend, Alistair Crotach the eighth McCleod chieftain, had entertained the King of Scotland here. When in Edinburgh, the King had asked McCleod what he thought of the table settings and candelabras at dinner. Great McCleod, in oaty Highland fashion had replied, "My Lord, if you come to my castle I will treat you to a feast with tables more grand than anything seen here and candles more numerous and beautiful." (He may talk like this to a king because in Scotland every man is considered the equal of every other; monarchs, princes and lords no better).

Eventually the King came to Dunvegan and the great clan Chief laid his feast under the night sky atop McCleod's Tables. "Tell me, Lord," he said, "Is this table not grander than anything you have and the stars not more splendid than any candles or candelabras at the Court?"

McLeod won his point.

Today there was no royal view, just sweeping rain mist, the kind that gets under clothes and into every nook and cranny. I climbed to the top of the larger Table and looked out over the edge to where the slope swept down towards the road. I wondered what it would be like to lean forward and just fly out into the free air. Suddenly, he appeared. I was startled.

"I didn't expect to see you here."

"Funny, I expected to find you," he said, without a hint of expression.

But it was a kind of joke, of course. I smiled appreciatively.

"Such a poor view," I mused.

"We may perhaps take that as a cue for a discussion about space and point of view."

"Well, how would you describe space?"

"Space is viewpoint and dimension."

"I need just a little bit more than that, please."

"There is always viewpoint. Without viewpoint there is nothing anyway. So the nature of space is directly related to Being, as you will see. But viewpoint must have points to view, dimension points or references, which lay out the space concept."

"I see. At least I think I do."

"Space is constructed from dimension points. As you are aware, Doctor, space dimensions travel off in opposite directions. You can go either way. But not so with time. Time is the peculiarity, the imposter. Again and again this is seen to be so."

"So the more dimension points you have, the more space you have?"

"Not strictly. More dimension points may imply a greater sense of space. But how much space is determined by how far apart the dimension points are."

"So remoteness and inaccessibility denote more space?"

"Precisely."

"But this discontinuity is felt as less space – or a denial of space. How do you explain that?"

"It's purely perception. The more you bring the outer periphery into view, the more space you have and the greater your Being."

"Do we need to consider multiple universes here; like last time?"

"Not really. These are the basic rules of space that would apply to any universe. Otherwise it would not be a universe!"

"You seem sure."

"It is unassailable, my friend."

"Well, you do surprise me," I let the sarcasm slip out in my tone of voice.

"I am serious. You cannot work your way around these properties of a universe."

"But multiple universes mean multiple spaces. Therefore none of them could be all-space."

"But every universe requires a separate Being, by definition almost."

"You say that space and Being is inseparable?"

"Think about it. If you had no space, you could not *recognize* Being, even if you had it."

"I suppose so."

"Of course space is also significant to flying. If you consider your body and yourself together to be located at an unusual point in space..."

"Say six feet off the ground!"

"Exactly. And if you maintained that position, or considered that you did, would that not be flying as you so earnestly crave it?"

"It would, except..."

"Except what?"

"It's no good me considering my body to be off the floor, if everyone else perceives it as stuck to the ground."

"You are close to invalidating your own reality again. We went through this earlier."

"No, not the same. I understand the three universes now. But surely if I fly in my universe and others simply believe it, this is an illusion? It need not agree with the accepted rules of the physical universe."

"Remember always the conjoint universe is the illusion. Science makes it seem more real. Yet science cannot explain any of the basic properties of this supposedly real universe. The measure of matter was once supposed to be *mass;* yet now science has conceded there are mass-less particles, matter without measure. How could this be?"

"Perhaps Sir Isaac Newton understood the confusions of science better than anyone."

"Isaac Newton?"

"He was probably the greatest physicist who ever lived. Yet he was deeply committed to exploring the occult and supernatural, to the horror of his contemporaries and biographers."

"Perhaps he was indeed close to discovering the ultimate secret of reality. At least he may have suspected where the truth lies."

"You know I have long had a pet theory that memory is space, rather than time."

"Explain."

"Well, place rather than time. That one's history is remembered more as a matter of where you were, than when. You know, 'the first time I was in Rome', rather than nineteen fifty five."

"That is wiser than you can possibly know. Where did you get this idea?"

"I don't remember. It just came to me one day. Why is it so important?"

"Time, as I have told you, is an illusion. But space is not. Space is a property of Being. Space is everything. A powerful soul we do not refer to as long-lasting, we say he or she is a BIG being."

The 1911 edition of *Encyclopaedia Brittanica* stated that space and time would only be explained when the mind itself was understood. Even then, expert thinking realized that time and space were properties of mind and not, as is supposed in science, properties of the physical universe. That only leaves matter and energy. Since matter itself, according to one Nobel laureate physicist, is only one billionth of the perceptible universe, it comes down mainly to energy… and information.

"Perhaps space and time are merely informational coding and not part of reality at all," I said out loud, not realizing I had been thinking to myself for a few moments.

"Doctor, once in a while you say something that makes it worthwhile to suffer the human condition!"

"Thanks," I said, with heavy irony.

"Be honoured, not insulted!"

"My choice?"

"Yours entirely."

"OK, I'll choose honour."

By this time the rain had become very heavy and we decided to descend from the cloud.

"I'm frightened of space. Does that mean I'm frightened of Being?"

"Probably. Explain yourself."

"When I was a kid I used to lie in bed and imagine what it meant for space to be infinite, to go on and on for ever. In my mind's eye I would travel outwards in a straight line and see myself journeying without end and that, no matter how far in front of me I could stretch, there was always infinitely more distance. It was a kind of challenge because I could never do it for more than a few minutes before becoming so frightened I broke out in a sweat and trembled so much I had to stop."

"I see."

"I know from conversations with friends that this experience is common. We all end up in the same place, which is to shut down thoughts of this type. They are too overwhelming to confront."

"That should not be, Doctor, if as you say so many people are hoping for greatness and escape. As I explained, space is Being; the more space you occupy, the greater your Being."

"I do see what you are saying. The problem is with the concept of infinity. People think they know what it means but it's just a mathematical abstraction, that isn't something real in the ordinary sense. So when we try to grasp onto it, we falter and tremble. But the mind alone, without the Self, can I think just grasp the infinite Cosmos. A famous writer G K Chesterton once joked that the Cosmos is just about the smallest hole into which the human mind will fit. Our mind fills the Cosmos, if you think about it for a moment."

"Mind but not Being, Doctor. This is different. You have revealed to me that the human mind can grasp the all-ness of known stars and galaxies, called the Cosmos, or Universe. Yet you cannot embrace it with your soul and Being. To own that space you must occupy it, not merely think of it."

"And I have to learn to do that, to be able to fly, right?"

"Correct."

"What happens if I can't?"

"You won't fly."

"Do you do workshops in failure, as well as personal empowerment?"

"I don't understand; is this humour?"

"Never mind," I said.

For the reader:

Try this space and Being exercise. Sit where you are relaxed and will not be disturbed. Go inside and take hold of your own viewpoint firmly. Now locate all 8 corners of the room. Concentrate on them, as your conscious focus. (Most people will not be able to do this without practice. If you can't, start with two corners, then four and so on.)

Do this for a week or more.

Then switch to feeling outwards towards other people. Reach out and out with your mind, reaching people in the nearby town, all over your country, including more and more beings. Get the feeling you connect with them all. You could affect the lives of every one of these billions of people.

Finally, the BIG space. Change the exercise to drifting off in conscious thought, on a tour of nearby planets and moons, then eventually the stars. Really see in your mind's eye that you are drifting through space towards your target. **Do not jump to a new location, travel to it,** all the millions and millions of miles that are necessary. You can go very fast if you wish but make sure you cover every mile of this journey.

10. Weighty Matters

That night I went to the village hall and listened to a bagpipe recital. The great performance of the evening was a blood-curdling piece called "The Lament for McSwann of Roag". Despite the title, this is no rest-in-peace tune; it's "bring me meat, you sons of dogs, and I'll avenge your wrongs, even from the further reaches of Hell…"

The tune's soul fury comes from a shrieking high G, which never fails to set my teeth on edge. Scottish pipe music is based on a strange scale, which is unlike anything else on Earth. It fits sweetly with the mournful pentatonic music, so beloved of the Celts, but if any stray note is introduced by the composer, it can be discordant indeed (though very musical, if worked with skill, nonetheless).

Like all the greatest tunes, McSwann is a McCrimmon piece and one wonders still where the likes of them are gone. McCrimmon is not really a Scottish name; it has been theorized they may have arrived as "Cremona", from the Italian musical city of that name and soon slipped into the "Mac" format, meaning "son of". Whatever their origin, they lasted less than two hundred years in their glory.

The last McCrimmon composer, Donald Ban, died on 17th February 1746. Lacking his ancestors' great compositional skills, he wrote an admittedly humble tune, but prophetically entitled "*Cha till mi tuilleadh*"

("I will never return") and went off to battle with his Chieftain, McLeod of McLeod. The events which followed were so singular they are worth reporting.

This was the time of Bonnie Prince Charlie's Jacobite rising (*Jacobus* is Latin for James – wannabe King James II - the Catholic pretender to the protestant throne of England). Bonnie Prince Charlie, James's foppish bisexual son, or "The Young Pretender" was lodging at Moy Hall, Lady Anne Mackintosh's home. Lady Anne received a spy message that a force of Hanoverian government soldiers, under Lord Loudon, was about to attack. Plucky twenty three year-old Lady Anne sent five of her staff out with guns to crash about and shout clan battle cries, to trick the government forces into thinking they were about to face the entire Jacobite army. The ruse worked and the pro-government army fled. The event became known, appropriately, as 'The Rout of Moy'.

Only five shots were fired in the fracas and only one man was hit, none other than Donald McCrimmon, who fell mortally wounded! It was the end of the line of composers. Truly Donald had the gift of "second sight" (prescience).

After the battle of Culloden in April of that year finally vanquished all Prince Charlie's hopes, Lady Anne was arrested and turned over to the care of her mother-in-law for a time. She was lucky to escape execution for treason. Later, Anne met the Duke of Cumberland, the young general commanding the Hanoverian army against the Scots, at a social event in London. The Duke, who incidentally was the son of King George II, asked her to dance to a pro-government tune and she returned the favour by asking him to dance to a Jacobite tune. George Frederick Handel's fine composition "See the Conquering Hero Comes!" commemorates Cumberland's victory. But in Scotland he was no hero; the plump youngster was known as the "Butcher of Culloden". His troops mutilated and killed more Highland soldiers after the final battle than during the actual fighting. Cumberland's most infamous act was ordering the firing of a church in which scores of defeated and exhausted Highlanders had taken shelter. All were burned to death.

History, they say, is written by the victors. But in this case, the romance of Prince Charlie's doomed and foolish attempt to win back his father's throne from the German King George of England, lives on in stories and songs of such courage, passion and beauty that it will never fade in human imagination. The tragedy is that Charlie's political folly led to Scot fighting Scot and that is often forgotten in the rush to prove the put-down of this misguided insurrection was an example of England's brutality to her northern neighbor. In truth it was, as usual, a religious war. Charlie, from the House Of Stuart, was a Papist and most clans did not want to go back to the fearful days of Catholic oppression and the burning of heretics. They fought just as gallantly on behalf of the protestant government in London as their fellow-countrymen did for the would-be usurper.

These thoughts were turning in my mind next morning, as I walked to Roag, along the west coast of Skye. The storm had cleared and the Sun shone, filled with brazen lure, in a wondrous blue sky. I have never been able to find out who the lamented McSwann was. Some worthy retainer of McLeod, no doubt. I continued my walk towards Idrigill Point, and came within sight of tall sea rocks known as McLeod's Maidens. They were no longer maidens, for sure. They had been ravished for aeons by the burly, lecherous tides of the Minch, sucking and chewing at their flanks. I lay on my back on a grassy slope, within sound of the waves, looking up at the arching sky.

"Dark thoughts for such a winsome day!" he said, greeting me.

The fairy sprawled on the grass beside me. His feet were sandaled and largely bare. I noted he had five toes, exactly like me. His ankles and foot anatomy seemed normal. I don't know if I expected knuckles, where wings might once have been attached or not. I remembered that Mercury, aka. Hermes, the messenger of the gods, had wings on his feet, not his back. That brought me to thinking of Hermes Trismegistus, the oracle sorcerer who is said to have founded alchemy. The word "hermetic" has survived in our language to mean matters arcane, occult, mysterious and supernatural.

It seemed appropriate. One didn't need wings here to think of flying in the magical sense.

"Tell me your perception of gravity," he said, in a surprising opening challenge.

"Well, it's a mystery. It works over great distances and nobody can say how. The Sun's pull keeps the Earth in orbit. But my question, as an ignorant layman…"

"Doctor, please…" His eyes closed with boredom, whether feigned or not.

"My question is: how does the Sun know the Earth is there? I mean it sounds silly. But this is action across a distance; action across a supposedly empty void. Empty! OK - science has invented gravitons to solve the problem, little particles, like light photons, that wander about, looking for stuff to link up with. Sounds pretty stupid and it is. Nobody has ever found a graviton."

"Perhaps, like the ether, gravity exists but doesn't exist," he smiled, his eyes still closed.

"Well, the truth is, we know nothing about the how of gravity. As I said, there are supposed to be these particles called gravitons. I think the idea is nonsense and they don't exist; something just dreamed up to patch over the yawning gaps in current theory. But if they did exist, it would be logical to postulate anti-gravitons; most particles come in pairs as a duality of opposites."

"Yes yes yes… but now let's have a little of what you call lateral thinking."

"Such as?"

"Stand with me now."

He opened his eyes and stood up. He summoned me to my feet.

"Why don't you try to think of yourself floating upside down and the Earth resting lightly on the soles of your feet."

I tried this and it wasn't easy at first. It took many attempts and possibly a quarter of an hour. When it came, I let out a yelp of embarrassed fright. It was an awful sensation! I was going to be crushed and my instinctive, jerking muscle reaction caused me to fall over like a fool!

When I had recovered, he asked, "Notice how those sheep are sticky and cling to the Earth!"

That wasn't easy either. But I got the idea and nodded. "And the crows over there; every time the wind puffs a little, they seem to fall off!" I said, excitedly.

The changes in sensation from just this simple exercise of mind and will was astonishing. I felt lighter, freer and ready to fly, if only I concentrated a little harder.

"Now push with your legs and try to push the Earth away from you! Think of the Earth moving down, not yourself going up."

I tried this and it was so easy; the huge planet was light as a feather. I kicked it away easily. Another shock to the senses. Was I really so trapped by this force that science insisted was there but could not demonstrate or prove to me? Gravity suddenly felt more like a phenomenon of consciousness than a physical reality. Perhaps that was why it was so elusive. Maybe the masses of reality we held in our heads were simply drawn together in some way contingent upon their creation by our thoughts. That attracting squeeze by the mind's limitations, we interpreted as gravity.

"Maybe gravity is all in the mind?" I said out loud.

"Very good doctor! Challenge earnestly everything you have been taught," he beamed.

"So one can overthrow it – without needing anti-gravity machines and all the clap trap that goes with them?"

He took my hand gently and held it.

Suddenly I found myself about twenty feet off the ground. He was there alongside, continuing to hold my hand. To this day I do not fully understand that Peter Pan moment. I think he controlled me in some hypnotic way and was making the point that it was indeed "all in the mind"; that if I changed my conscious view, I could change my relationship to gravity.

I don't think we flew in the sense of magical flying.

But that brought back the nagging, inescapable question: was not all magical flying merely in the mind? Just a phenomenon of the personal universe?

Back on the ground I sighed. Not long ago I could not have imagined such thoughts. Now I was engaged deeply with this critical exploration of the self and reality.

He nodded. I understood quite clearly, without words, that it was to say: OK to acknowledge your attainment - give yourself a pat on the back.

Walking back towards the village of Roag, we continued to talk.

"Gravity, of course, is something real in the Newtonian world," I announced. "That's what made Newton famous. But quantum physics seems to be susceptible to the intrusion of thought, of conscious perception. Gravity has no place in quantum mechanics."

"Doctor, will you drop these intellectual profanations for a while. I am asking you to BE, to live and perceive gloriously. All you seem to want to do is fill your experiences with hollow prattlings, such as you term science."

"Science, of course, really means simply knowledge, from the Latin scientiae, to know, so real knowledge, such as you are …"

"Shut UP!"

He had stopped and stared at me quite indignantly.

"Stand still. You must be still. The spirit is always still."

I attempted to stand still, without flinching.

"Relax. I don't mean stillness of the body. I mean stillness of the mind. Calm in the heart, soul, whatever you want to call it."

I tried again.

"Now without closing your eyes, stop perceiving the outer scene. Instead reach out for the imagined corners of this morning. Think of the morning as you hold it within."

I tried hard.

"You do not need to embarrass yourself – or me," he added as an afterthought, "By attempting to define verbally what you feel. Merely try this exercise, as I ask. You will notice, I am sure, that the further you reach out, the greater your perception of the morning, the greater is the space of your Being."

I nodded. I could grasp this intellectually but I sort of felt it too. He was actually my guru. Because, with his guiding presence, I could sense and experience things I probably could not otherwise have done. Merely having been told such things would not suffice. I felt I understood that much at least.

It was a morning of transformation.

"You are this day!" he said.

My heart sang as the truth of it dawned.

Suddenly the sky was clearer and bluer than ever in my life, the sounds crisper, the sights sweeter and the smells of a Hebridean summer day tormented my senses with the delicate fragrances of heather, flowers and the tangled sea. I felt I could detect the vibrations of birds' wings beating the air, ever so many of them, in ever so distant places, all over the world, from humming birds to eagles, from ducks to kingfishers. And I knew I was not imagining this strange sensation. I did not need to challenge my intellect.

It was a breakthrough.

For The Reader:

Walk around for a time and look at the people or animals. Notice they are heavy and seem to stick to the Earth's surface.

Try the exercise in which you alter your perceptions, so as to feel yourself upside down and the Earth as resting upon your feet, above you. This is hard but you will get it if you persist.

Flex your knees slightly and then push the Earth firmly away from you. Repeat this over and over, striving for the sensation that the Earth moves and you do not. Notice how light you feel!

Stop and look at your day, your very day. Think beyond our planet, beyond the solar system and the galaxies. Go as far as you like outwards and notice that you cannot find any part of this existence called "today" of which you are not already a part, as soon as you connect with it!

If you can handle it, seek outwards in time, go backwards and forwards, into the deep past, into the future, as far as your mind can perceive. Notice too that you are part of all time. It has no reality without you. Tell yourself you are truly GREAT.

Ends.

11. The Mystical Boson

When I got home I grabbed the first chance I could to take my friend Charles for a coffee and start pumping him for some understanding of what science thinks about weight and what gravity really means. Charles was from the Physics Department but we met mainly to play chess and talk about philosophy.

I asked him about the current state of play in physics and how the mysterious force of gravity was viewed, hoping to get an insight that somebody else had missed. A silly notion, of course. But I was, by now, gripped by the mystery of magical flying.

"Funny you should ask," Charles started off. "There is a radical new theory up, that could explain the nature of inertia, abolish gravity and, just possibly, lead to bizarre new forms of spacecraft propulsion."

"I'll just settle for why humans can't fly and why Peter Pan could!" I joked. It was close to the bone but he didn't know that.

"Well, that's a question of mass. But we don't know what mass is. Not a clue!"

"It's what makes a loaded shopping trolley hard to get moving," I said.

"No, that's inertia. It's related to mass, of course. Or perhaps, mass is what makes a bag of sugar or a grand piano weigh what they do, instead of floating away on the air currents. Either way, the origin of mass is one of Mother Nature's deepest mysteries."

"Mass is not the same as weight. I can remember that from school."

"Right."

"I thought I read somewhere that mass is a property of the hypothetical particle, a Higgs boson? Isn't the Higgs boson supposed to create mass. The more of them stick to stuff, the more mass it has?"

"So they say."

"Trouble is, nobody has ever seen a Higgs boson! A strange theory, that's based on something that doesn't exist..." I pointed out.

"Ahh, the mystical Higgs boson," he said, with an almost reverential overtone. I knew he was being facetious. "Some call it the God-particle..."

Yes, I'd heard that too.

"Of course you know the Higgs boson has been found?" he said, deadly serious for a moment.

I raised my eyebrows involuntarily. I knew they had been building the Large Hadron Collider at CERN in Switzerland to try and demonstrate this elusive particle. But I'd never heard of any breakthrough, which would surely have hit the popular press, as well as science journals.

"Scientists the world over have hailed the discovery as a tremendous advancement for fundamental physics, but have expressed surprise at some of the particles unique attributes. Previous estimates by scientists had the particle pegged at about one millionth of a nanometer. Instead, it turns out it's about the size of a ping-pong ball and bright green. It was discovered behind the cushions on the family sofa by a kid in Topeka, Kansas, while looking for the remote control to the TV. He thought it was a gobstopper..."

I laughed. But it was a pity he couldn't be serious for a moment. I really was interested.

"Now scientists all over the country over have been applying for grants to begin a nation-wide search for any evidence of the missing dark matter hiding behind old boxes in garages," Charles went on, mainly for his own amusement. "The European Union has just approved funding to build a gigantic, thirteen kilometre-wide loveseat in hopes of discovering the even more elusive gluon under the cushions."

"The gluon?" I was suspicious this was just another joke. I knew the particle zoo had grown apace over the decades but this seemed a little too silly.

"Never mind," he said. "Another shot of caffeine and I'll tell you about the new theory of gravity, as promised."

I was happy to oblige him.

"So," I asked when we settled down again. "How can these physicists claim they have discovered the origin of mass when their proposed mechanism fails to explain the very things that make it what it is?"

"Well, as Bill Clinton might say, it all depends on what you mean by mass," replied Charles, after a mouthful of latte. "When these particle physicists speak of mass, they are not thinking in terms of inertia or weight. Matter is just a concentrated form of energy. We talk about the two as equivalent; an equivalence embodied in Einstein's famous equation E= mc2. So in this sense, the mass of a subatomic particle is a measure of the amount of energy it contains. The Higgs can account for that, at least partly."

"But I still don't see how the Higgs boson mechanism explains why mass, or its energy equivalent, resists motion or reacts to gravity.

"It doesn't," Charles replied dryly.

"So?"

"I'm getting to that. The interesting new model says that inertia and gravity could be manifestations of far more familiar effects. When you lift that sack of potatoes or shove your shopping trolley, the forces you feel might be plain old electricity and magnetism."

"Electromagnetism? No way!"

"Whether you call this an explanation of mass is a matter of taste, I guess. I would be inclined to say no, since it doesn't simplify the description of mass, nor suggest testable new properties of mass."

Now I was getting puzzled.

"Let me ask you if you know what the quantum vacuum is?" Charles asked.

"It's supposed to be a sea of energy. I heard Richard Feynman say there was enough energy in a cubic meter of vacuum to boil all the world's oceans."

"Exactly, so it's not really a vacuum. Now, the best understood of all energy fields is the electromagnetic field, and it affects us constantly -- our bodies are held together by electromagnetic forces, and light is an oscillation in the electromagnetic field."

"Go on, I'm with you… I think."

"So rather than being empty, the vacuum is a choppy sea of randomly fluctuating electromagnetic waves. We don't see or feel them because they pop in and out of existence incredibly quickly, appearing only for a split second."

He took another sip of latte. "These fleeting apparitions are called virtual particles. In the mid-1970s, professor Paul Davies…"

"The man who wrote *The Mind Of God!*"

"Him… Davies and a guy called Bill Unruh realized that an observer accelerated through the quantum vacuum should be bathed in electromagnetic radiation." The quantum vacuum becomes a real and detectable thing. You still following?"

"Yes, I think so…"

"Well, what if this radiation exerted a retarding force?"

"Ah," I said, starting to catch on. "Like the Sun's radiation throws out charged particles which push on a comet and makes its particles stream outwards. That's electromagnetic radiation."

"Exactly. Now think for a minute. This electromagnetic drag, if it exists, certainly sounds like inertia, doesn't it?"

"For an object at rest, yes. But not for something already moving. Inertia says a moving object resists change, including slowing down…" I felt sure I'd outsmarted him there. This was Isaac Newton's First Law Of Motion.

"No, this still works. Forget about Newton and think about it. Let's just suppose that the vacuum field energies are coming up behind the object traveling. They push it along and would resist you trying to slow the object down, right?"

I realized he was correct.

"So now we have inertia and mass as two sides of the same thing, right?" he went on.

Again I nodded. This much was high school stuff.

"Now what if the vacuum energy radiations could also account for gravitational mass too? The idea of linking gravity with the vacuum was suggested by Russian physicist Andrei Sakharov and has been developed recently by Puthoff. This latest theory is an attempt to link all these ideas into something new and cohesive."

"But what about Einstein's theory that gravity was just a curvature of space. That's always been accepted, since it predicts astronomical observations so accurately?"

"That's right. Einstein's theory of general relativity already explains gravity beautifully in terms of the warping of space-time by matter, so this electromagnetic force description, if it's correct, ought to be compatible with this new quantum-vacuum picture. Remember Einstein's curved space can only be inferred from the bending of the paths of light rays. But supposing the vacuum could refractively bend light paths, just as a piece of glass or the surface of water does when light enters or leaves it. "

"Then you wouldn't need curved space to explain what was going on?" I joined in.

"You nailed it. Put it another way: the warping of space might be equivalent to a variation in the refractive index of the quantum vacuum, like a lens which also bends light."

"So space would still appear to be curved?"

"Exactly. In this way, all the mathematics of general relativity could stay, intact, since space-time would still look as if it were warped. But we just wouldn't need gravity." He turned to his coffee as if he was done.

But I wasn't yet satisfied. I might have been the first human ever to beat gravity. Or I might have been deluded the previous week in Skye. But I wanted to know as much about this as possible.

"I still don't see how that explains mass. Or how a lack of mass could come about. You hinted we could maybe get free of gravity?"

Charles sighed archly. But he was soon up and running again. "You need to understand we recognize three types of mass: inertial mass, the resistance to change; gravitational mass, the effect you call weight; and that just leaves rest mass, the kind of mass that's equivalent to energy. According to this new theory, the Higgs boson might not be needed to explain rest mass at all.

"Are you saying that if gravitational and inertial mass emerge from the vacuum, perhaps we could take control of them? Or at least take control of the energy equivalents?"

"There are lots of implications, yes. It might be possible to cancel mass altogether, creating an inertia-less drive that could accelerate a spaceship to nearly the speed of light in the blink of an eye."

"A human being might fly by magic?" I tested him, warily.

"If you like. But to do this we would have to blow a bubble in the vacuum, so to speak, to exclude quantum fluctuations from a region where there is matter…"

"Such as on Earth?"

He nodded.

That made me doubtful. "Nature abhors a vacuum; isn't that what they say?"

"It's not true," Charles snorted. "However, She may abhor a vacuum in the vacuum!"

That night I went to bed with my head aching with ideas.

Maybe there isn't a Higgs boson. But what about bringing in tachyons for this electro-magnetic radiation theory, instead of protons? I asked myself. Tachyons are even more mystical and other-worldly than the Higgs boson. Not a God particle but the Devil particle maybe… If a tachyon exists at all, it must only travel *faster than light*.

Apart from other oddities, the equations for energy and momentum for such particles reveal that tachyons would accelerate as they lose energy and slow down if they were given energy. This leads to one of the most peculiar characteristics of tachyons: their possession of negative energy. But negative energy, like the square root of minus one, is just a concept. It doesn't exist, does it?

More peculiar still, such particles will seem to travel backward in time.

The implications of such behavior were noticed by Richard Tolman as early as 1917 in what has come to be known as Tolman's Paradox, namely, that communication with the past is possible. So if the mass eliminating effect of inertia drag from the vacuum that Charles was talking about was applied using tachyons, instead of "real" particles, would everything go in reverse?

By interacting with tachyons, a body would be lose mass or perhaps even become weightless altogether? That might work for me…

The trouble is, I could reason out, that tachyons working through a vacuum would be incredibly weak.

Then I remembered reading a Russian paper that stated, declaratively, that the motion of tachyons at speeds of faster than light would generate gravity waves. But then the same paper said that all tachyons must have been used up, or lost to our universe, in the first few seconds after the supposed Big Bang.

I felt very confused!

I decided that, after all, advanced physics, no matter how mystical in nature, might not have the answers I was looking for. The fairy had said it would take a shift in consciousness, hadn't he, not a doctorate in particle physics?

For the reader:

Try the advanced tachyon anti-telephone "thought experiment". You can find it on the Internet.

A tachyonic anti-telephone is a hypothetical device that could theoretically be used to send signals into one's own past. R. C. Tolman first thought of it in 1917. You have to figure out how it can be done without destroying basic causality. In other words you can't go back and kill your own grandfather, because then your father would not have been born and then you could not be here!

But it is possible for different observers at different times to see different aspects of causality. Clue: a real particle moving backward in time is observed to be a forward moving anti-particle, so no observer interprets this as time.

12. A Wild Ride Through The Mind Of God

Some of the oldest rocks on planet Earth come to the surface on Skye, a fact which may explain its unique mysterious energies. At the north eastern end of the island is a long promontory which is dominated by a huge geological fault, a land slip aeons ago, which has resulted in the eastern side of the promontory being several hundred feet below the scarp to the west. Overlooking the township of Staffin, a strange rock formation has come into being, wrought and twisted by the mysterious forces of nature, known as the Quirang.

In its many tortured and grotesque forms, men have discovered the likeness of a castle, a prison, a cathedral spire and a table. But there are many more crooked pillars, towers and crenellations which defy the power of human imagination to interpret. The whole forms a labyrinth of such proportions that it was said that in the old days of clan warfare, when the enemy was on the rampage, cattle, wives and children were hidden here for safety. Over the last one and a half centuries, a yearly shinty match has been played hundreds of feet up in the air, on the grassy flat top of The Table (*Am Bord*).

If you go to the Quirang alone, do not go in mist. The eeriness of the place is oppressive and will rekindle primaeval fears of the Devil and the hounds of Hell. Hereabouts, one can sense, the Underworld comes close to the surface and some say cracks open on certain dark and moonless nights, to allow evil spirits to emerge from beneath the ground and dance in a frenzy for a few hours. For the sake of your immortal soul, be sure you are not present when it happens.

A completely different view is to be had ascending from the west, to the edge of the eastward scarp at its highest point, *Ben A'Siga*. One is entirely in an upland vale under the arching sky. I did so one day during my flying project and I was happy to be there alone, looking down on the Quirang, far below. The menace, such as it was, did not extend to my high perch.

I had not yet been to see the fairy on this trip north.

Lying in the afternoon sun on the summit of *Ben A'Siga*, I tried to vizualize space in a different way. I let my mind drift upwards and outwards from the earth, off into the remote blue of the heavens. It was easy to gain the sense of infinity, though I played once more with the idea it was just a construct of consciousness and had no real meaning, except in the world of mathematics. After all, we could talk about an infinite number of apples or pebbles on a beach. But we were not able to *experience* an infinite number of any object; only about three dozen apples at once and doubtless not more than a few bucketfuls of pebbles, before it all became conceptual mush.

Perhaps space was like that – infinite and yet meaningless. Just an idea that had no root. There was no need to be afraid of infinite distance because it didn't exist. But then, isn't that what the fairy was saying all along, that *there is no universe as such,* outside our minds?

My thoughts were interrupted when I spied an eagle, a huge golden eagle. He hovered close and I kept still. The idea suddenly came to me that he had come to see me, personally.

I was "invited" by the eagle to fly with him. An eagle is my totem animal, I knew that. I was to see the truth through his eyes.

The eagle seemed to be hovering, as if waiting for me to climb aboard. Then, in a blink, I got the idea and I knew I was seeing through the bird's eyes; I could see myself far below, a small figure on the edge of the abyss. We circled higher and higher and were soon lifted up into cloud. I grappled with the shift of viewpoint forced on me and did not find this easy. I could see nothing for a time. I felt queasy.

It was reminiscent of scenes from the lovely movie "The Emerald Forest" in which characters snort hallucinogens and are then transported over the ether to remote places, with the All-Seeing Eye of wisdom, which is that of a bird flying.

In its many forms, the All-Seeing Eye surfaces in several of Man's philosophical systems. In ancient Egypt, there was a school that taught disciples to communicate through telepathy, dominate the basic instincts and remember their past lives in order to learn from the past incarnations. It was the mystery school of the Eye of Horus and it had the All-Seeing Eye as its symbol.

Always the eye has symbolized a tool to find the truth in a world full of contrasts, and the truth is found when one has the ability to reunite the contrasts and understand all duality like two sides of the same thing. One side cannot exist without the other.

In the ancient mystery school, the Eye of Horus was broken into six different symbols, each of them representing one among the seven steps that leads to full consciousness, described in so many cultures. The seventh symbol is the Eye itself, which is the union of all the other six, meaning that one reaches God once he has gone through all the six levels of consciousness.

Since Egyptians believed that a person needs approximately seven hundred incarnations in order to understand God and all creation—and this is the purpose of every human being, according to ancient Egyptian tradition—the soul that has achieved the wisdom and knowledge which is a result of many lives in different bodies.

The Eye of Horus, then, is the eye of the person who has achieved enlightenment through various incarnations and has learned the mystery of God. Gnostic studies suggest that Horus is the same as the Holy Spirit of Christianity, Shiva of Hinduism and Sangha of Buddhism.

Enlightenment in Ancient Egypt was represented as a falcon, as the falcon they believed, has the best vision among animals. Horus is the falcon god. Today, I got me an eagle! It was like being upgraded to first-class on an airline flight. Nothing, in my world-view, has the power, the vision, the prescience, the majesty of an eagle.

I was mightily honored.

But, whereas they got seven years for every grade in the Eye of Horus School of Mystery, I was grabbed and thrust into it in just a matter of minutes. Moreover, this was the cold northern climes of Scotland, not a warm, sunny desert.

I clung on for dear life and wondered what was going to happen.

When the mist finally cleared to permit a view, what I saw below shook me to my core. It was definitely not Skye, nor were there hills and valleys; not even Scotland. I was on a glorious cruise above all earthly realities—I could see whole worlds passing below, like wildebeest trekking on the plains, universe after universe, all the same, yet each and every one totally different.

I couldn't help wondering how did the Eagle stay aloft? What was he flying in? This was not Earth atmosphere any longer.

It was breathtaking, yet violently beautiful, taking me beyond the reaches of any neurological experience I had ever had. I began to feel a sense of the identity of divine being, with all-knowing powers, that we had lost in ages past.

I lost count of the universes which paraded themselves invitingly before me. Each one was different; one was without light, one without form, another was ever-changing, with the laws of physics twisting and twirling like a kaleidoscopic image. I saw possibility after possibility.

I got the happy thought of beings a tourist inside the mind of God, traveling on a day-pass from the everyday realm of human reason! Wow!

Best of all, I detected a current, call it an essence of reality, running through all, and that was the element of Love. Indeed, beyond an element, it was a law, a condition of every universe everyone could ever create, imagine or believe in: that whatever IS, whatever Being comes into contact with a universe, no matter how divergent the behaviors, that love rules all, love was more than physics, love was its own universe, a superordinant flow that not only existed in every universe, but held it in check, kept it welcoming, made everything seem just wonderful.

I knew, of course, this was all part of my training. Somewhere, the fairy was behind this encounter. I was being shown the wildness of realities unknown and infinite possibilities that took me to the boundaries of reason and far, far beyond.

My mentor may have strange methods but he did seem to be expanding my consciousness in vast and enthralling ways.

"Very good, Doctor."

I looked around for the voice but I could see no-one, of course. Then it came to me.

He was the eagle!

The realization brought me to earth with a bump and I saw once again from my own eyes, from a human body clinging feebly to the ground on the hill top. I was partly vexed at him, for the trick, and partly ecstatic from the thrill of what I had just enjoyed.

The eagle swooped low over my perch and then vanished out of sight among the towers and bastions of the precipice.

Next day I tackled him about the deception.

"I fell for your trick, being a bird."

"I don't know what you are talking about."

"You.. You were the eagle."

"I was not!" He sounded most indignant.

"But, you spoke to me."

"The universe may have spoken to you, or your own inner light. But it wasn't me."

"Whatever it was, I flew like a bird."

"Interesting Doctor. But you don't want to be a bird. They fly by the laws of physics. That is not magical flying."

It was somewhat deflating.

"I have an interesting observation you, Doctor, something you might like to try when you are alone in your room perhaps. You do not even need to carry out the action, just imagine yourself doing it."

"A thought experiment?"

"If you say so. Consider yourself walking around the room you are in: what exact action would you take? Picture yourself walking round the room."

It didn't seem difficult, I was practically doing it as he spoke.

"You will note that you did not truly *walk around the room* at all, you merely walked around near the edge, within the confines of the walls, without touching them, right?"

"Agreed."

"Then walk around the room once more."

I nodded when I had done this too.

"Now you have walked round the entire universe."

I'm sure I looked baffled.

"True, you were a long way in from the edge but the event was essentially the same."

"Is this a trick?"

"You must try it yourself and see."

For the reader:

Imagine you are flying and seeing through the eyes of an eagle. You may also expand your consciousness by taking up the being of a chair, a tree or a stone. Actually be that object and work your way into how it feels.

Then try walking round the universe, exactly as the fairy instructed. See if you can judge how far from the edge you may be!

Can you perceive the wisdom of this simple re-framing of experience?

13. The Time Before Time

"You are very patient with my enquiries," I found myself saying at a later meeting.

"Patience is not a concern for us," he replied.

"Yes, I suppose. You immortals must have infinite amounts of time."

"No, you are mistaken. The whole point is that we don't have any time. It's meaningless."

I must have looked surprised.

"Time is the basic illusion. When you are free of that, most secrets of the universe will surrender."

"I don't understand."

"Take flying that you so earnestly desire. If you were to leap into the air you would be flying, even if you were back on the ground again in a split second. But if you were to hang there and time stand still, so that you did not fall back quickly, would that not be flying as you desire it?"

"Yes, it would."

"Well then, time is the key, as it is to many things."

"So flying is really just conquering time?"

"No, I'm not saying that. But conquering time is freeing yourself from all the limitations of what humans are pleased to call the real world. Do you not see that without time, space surrenders?"

"Because I could just be in every place at once, visit them all in turn but all at the same time? And I could be up in the air at the same time as standing on the ground?"

"Exactly."

"Wow! This really is something new for me."

I suddenly began to feel very strange, disconnected. The world opened out in a completely new way. It was a wide oceanic feeling, containing all elements of everything and accompanied by a wonderful new emotion that I can only describe as achingly beautiful, bitterly sweet. It was almost too much to endure; I went into a kind of trance.

I don't know how long I stayed in this reverie but when I came to, he was still sitting there patiently, smiling and watching me, like a tender parent.

"Let us take this interesting metaphor you call time, Doctor, and work with it as a tool. You will see that it contains the essence of its own destruction, that will liquify and dissolve all these notions that seem such a barrier to you."

"You make it sound like digestive enzymes."

"Your language, Doctor, your language. I will make for you more time, so much that you will not be able to deal with it. And so you will come to have less of it."

"How do you mean?" I was completely mystified by this awesome claim and could not guess what he meant.

"I will show you. Are you comfortable, sitting thus?"

"I'm fine."

"Close your eyes and allow yourself to turn inwards, simply relax."

"Huh-hmmm."

"Now drift back to some pleasant memory but actually *be there*, not simply recalling it."

"This is hypnotic reverie, right?" I had done some hypnotism and it didn't seem any different to me.

"Doctor, please refrain from being a spectator to yourself and using technical labels. Simply BE — and do what I ask you."

"It isn't easy."

"Ignore the mind chatter and simply detach from present reality. The universe I want you to examine is within, not out here."

"Well, I'm in alpha, anyway, semi-aware of the environment."

"Doctor, please!"

"Sorry."

"I promise you there are no words for where you are going."

Eventually I settled down and was able to ignore the outside environment, though fully aware of where I was and what I was doing. A memory rose up of a day on the beach when I was a child, long before adult values had encroached and altered my world view from fun to anxiety. It was very pleasant to recall, from the present-day perspective. I described it to my transcendental therapist.

"Now go earlier," he instructed, once he was sure I was back there in time.

Well, I know about prenatal memories and was soon into one of those. Father and mother making love, I think. A bit of a bumpy ride.

"Earlier," he kept saying.

Now as it happens, I have quite good past life recall. I have never had any problem with reincarnation. To me, the weird idea is that you only live once. We spent the next two hours looking at mediaeval knights, Vikings, then Roman gladiators. Several incarnations were in eighth century China, as a monk, seeking enlightenment, but I lapsed after that; it was certainly not all upwards towards better things. I had been lover, bandit, prince, murderer and philosopher. There is no doubt our pasts are pretty macabre and despicable. I died many times, usually violently and stupidly. But then who wants to die in bed? When you know you will come around again, death has less fears and this tends to make you reckless!

Earlier and earlier, he always wanted more.

"I've found a memory of being eaten by a sabre-tooth tiger."

"Far too recent. Go back, back and back."

At first I didn't believe this was possible but, surprisingly, I saw a clam on a distant seashore, millions of years ago, and knew it was me. Weird. As the sea washed it, it oozed water from the corners of its maw and I knew with certainty these were the first tears I shed on Earth!

"Earlier," he urged. As I protested, he started to bang his stick and raise his voice. "Come on, Doctor, you're not trying. Demand that your unconscious mind open out. There is much more there."

"Listen, are you really a fairy or some kind of freak New Age guru?"

"Shut up, please and concentrate."

"I can't, this is crazy."

"Do it!" he snapped, bang bang bang with the stick.

It was at this moment I began to wish I had channelled one of those voices that spoke in vague comfortable metaphors, instead of meeting this demanding irascible character!

"How, for heaven's sake?"

"You are the source, the conscious power. Your inner psyche will deliver you whatever you ask of it. Just say earlier."

"I see a silver spaceship. Say, what is this?"

"Just continue."

"It's thousands of millions of years ago. This isn't planet Earth."

"Good, we have progress. Return, return. Keep going back."

The next thing I found was a strange world, dark and secretive, with lush vegetation. The buildings were not unlike present-day Germany. The figures all had white suits with pink candy-stripes. They were a clever race and had developed atomic power. They looked beautiful, somehow, though far from human. It was poignant to go back. I suddenly found myself crying and had to excuse this lapse.

"Pay no attention, Doctor. This is but emotion."

"It was about a billion years ago, I think."

"Once again, what lies earlier?"

"There are many worlds before this. I've just had an idea. Maybe the place called Atlantis was not a lost continent of Earth at all but some other planet where we once lived and were wise and happy. People remember the time and make up the metaphor of it sinking into the sea, to explain why it can't be found here on Earth. There just isn't enough geological time on Earth to lose a whole continent."

"Will you please stop complicating matters by your insistence on imposing intellectualism on our quest. The mind has nothing to offer this project, beyond being the doorway to understanding. The mind itself contains *nothing whatever* that we shall be needing in the pursuit of spiritual power."

"But it's possible, you must admit?"

"Doctor, please! One thing at once. The human mind is a glorious thing, in that it can embrace so many ideas of such enormous scope and diversity. But it is virtually non-functional when it comes to fully grasping one simple idea." He was starting to sound weary of my ramblings. "Just keep returning, earlier. Let your consciousness seek out the darkest corners of time and visit those too. It is all there."

I found myself suddenly back a hundred billion years, hovering above a pretty green-blue planet, rather like our earth, though I knew it was not.

"This is ridiculous. It is before the Big Bang."

"Consciousness did not have a Big Bang, Doctor. It merely is, was and always will be."

"But what about the physical universe?"

"Which physical universe?"

"Ah, I get it."

"Go back, further back."

"Are you kidding?"

"Just do as I ask, please."

I don't know how much time lapsed in Earth hours but I had soon squandered huge segments of eternity and was back at eight quadrillion years. The Universe was now very dark and young; it seemed quite plastic and fluid.

"This is my home universe, it's created by me, exactly as you said!" I told him excitedly. "Other peoples' universes are in the vicinity but not fused with mine, at least not fully. Everything is just starting to coalesce."

"Do you now understand, Doctor?"

"Yes, yes! This is the start of the physical universe, as we all agree and accept the common reality."

If this had been a taped session on playback, I would probably have diagnosed myself as totally insane at this point, listening to what I was saying. It was the ravings of an idiot. Yet everything seemed entirely logical, coherent and easy to understand.

"Now, what lies before this?" demanded the fairy, unrelenting.

"How can there be anything before this?"

"Look!" He banged his stick hard.

"I can't see anything."

"Try harder!" Bang bang bang.

"But this is the dawn of time! How *can* there be anything earlier?"

"Think!" he yelled, staring straight into my eyeballs, inches away, like an irate army drill sergeant.

The pressure was too much. I burst out sobbing and could not control myself. "I don't understand, I don't know what you're driving at," I said amongst my tears.

"Yes you do, Doctor, you know the answer to this question. Trust me."

I shook my head and looked down.

"What lies earlier? Reach for it, think man!"

I kept shaking my head, as bewildered as ever. Then, in the midst of my confusion and despair, like a phantom of beauty rising out of the morning mist, the answer came to me.

"It's me! I'm there. It's *me*... before time begins!"

He relaxed and smiled.

"We have a result, eh, Doctor?"

I felt like a wrung out flannel.

"All this consciousness is inside me?"

"No, Doctor, this consciousness **is** you. There is no other awareness that you need concern yourself with, if we are to conquer the physical universe."

I cannot remember how I got back to my lodgings that day. I felt as weak and insubstantial as vapour. My body looked almost transparent. Yet somehow it impinged on the physical world enough to unlock the door to my room.

I collapsed on the bed in a swoon.

For the reader:

If you haven't done a great deal of past life work, such a deep time experience as this will not be available to you. You may have to clean up a lot of this-lifetime memories, before the Tunnels of Time will open to you. You may consider joining my **Tunnels Of Time** project; you may even learn to do for your friends what the fairy did with me (without being so bossy!).

If you have not had a past life experience at all, find a practitioner and get one. Then you will understand the framework of this section far better.

In the meantime: try this experiment in stretching Time, from the cue above. Stand on a small step or low platform and jump off. Contemplate the split second experience as you fall. Now jump repeatedly and see if you can draw out the sensation of falling. How much consciousness can you put in that gap? A result would be a delayed sense of arrival to the floor, no matter how slight a sensation. You will be aware that Time is fairly subjective.

Note: The famous dancer Nijinsky was reputedly able to stay in the air longer than anyone in the history of dance. It was said of him that he did not jump any higher but "came down more slowly".

If we could stretch coming down to as long as we wished, wouldn't that be flying?

14. The Memory Problem

Next day I was quite recovered and decided on a walk south of the village of Kilmuir, where Flora MacDonald, saviour of Bonnie Prince Charlie, lies buried. On the lands to the south, between the road and the sea's edge there are a number of places of interest. Monkstadt House, home of the MacDonald chieftain at the time of the 1745 rising, now lies in ruins and the north westerly wind whistles through the rooms where once Flora and the Prince spent the night, after landing from South Uist. History does not record if they were lovers on their daring journey of escape but the libertine behaviour of the bisexual Prince, who bedded regularly with two- and threesomes of either sex, makes it seem more than likely.

The house takes its name (German: "*monk's town*") from a small monastic community formerly sited on the loch nearby. On what was a small island in the middle of a loch are the remains of several beehive shaped monastic dwellings, said to have been built by St Columba. According to legend, the last Norseman in Skye was killed on the island.

Loch Chaluim Chille, or St Columba's Loch in English, is now drained (1824) but was some two miles in length. No sooner was the arduous task of reclamation completed by the hopeful crofters, than the rapacious landlord appropriated the new land for himself. One wonders why the Scots complain so bitterly of the English, when it was largely the greed of Scottish barons and landlords who drove off their own folk, in favour of lucrative sheep. All over the north the pattern was repeated. The Highlands were cleared - but to the great benefit of the Americas, which gained a decent hard-working people—and thereby a chain of hamburger stores which is forever a watchword for enterprise and fortune!

Further south I came to the hamlet of Skudaborg with its striking Pictish broch. The Picts were probably the nearest we had to an aboriginal people in Britain, before the Romans drove them back to Caledonia in the north. Their name is said to derive from the Roman *Pictii*, meaning "painted" people. This supposes they were tattooed but I think dyed with woad is simpler and more likely.

I somehow knew I would find him there. My hunch was correct.

"I have been here before," I told him. "This fortification is very old, say about three thousand years. Yet there is a puzzle."

"Which is?"

"The outer face of the stones here have been fused by some great heat, a process we call vitrification."

"Why is that such a problem to you?"

"Because the temperatures required to make it happen are enormous. Wood fires could not possibly generate sufficient heat. Science has no explanation of how this took place, yet it did. Here is the evidence on Skye."

"Ah, and you were wondering, in the modern fashion, whether it may have been caused by an atomic blast from an ancient rocket ship visiting the Earth?"

"Well, after yesterday, I believe it could have happened. The recall was good, strong and clear, with the exact same qualities of memory. No different to remembering yesterday, or one year ago."

"You accept these memories are true?"

"I do. What I have trouble accepting is how or why I have been carrying around the baggage for such aeons of time!"

"The mystery is not memory but time itself. Have I not said that if I made more time for you, you would have less of it?"

"You did."

"Well?"

"It's true. Despite opening up all those huge tracts of the past, time seems less important."

"But the most valuable recollection, surely, is a time before time?"

"Absolutely. That accords very well with what I read of the Vedas. But at what stage did beings switch to collecting these memories and why?"

"In the beginning we were all-powerful, all-seeing, all-knowing; memory was pointless. Only when more limited powers had been assumed would beings need memory, as such."

I wonder what Freud would have made of this conversation!

"So super beings would not need a mind?"

"Strictly not. The difference between Man, the spirit and more highly developed entities, is that we do not need to clutter our psychic space with details of memory, identity, learning, experience and so on. If we want to know something, we just 'know it'."

"Grok!"

"Pardon?"

"Grok. It was a term in vogue in the sixties, from a science fiction classic book by Robert Heinlein called *Stranger In A Strange Land*. The man from Mars just took an all-knowing imprint of something, which he called to 'grok'. He was a demi-god, from the perspective of Earth people. The point of the story, I think, was to teach us something about ourselves."

"But no hint that's what Man once was?"

"It was only a story, remember. Mind you, science fiction doesn't seem quite so fictional after those whole-time memories of yesterday. Maybe authors are just vaguely remembering something when they suppose they are making it all up!"

"I have never read this or any other literature. But I think I understand what you are saying."

"So memory is the fill-in blank, to remind us who we are and where we come from, when we lose the power of total knowing?"

"That is the sad truth."

"And I just know you are going to tell me that to fly I am going to need to transcend memory too?"

"But of course. Most memory is disempowering; even the existence and need of memory is disempowering."

"But memory is learning and knowledge! How can you say such things?"

"The fact remains that it is memory, this knowledge, as you call it, of what you are, that keeps you earth bound. It would be better to forget your powerless state, not constantly remember it."

"Why can't Man use memories to rekindle the power of the past, to recall once again what it was like to be gods and goddesses? It should work both ways."

"Alas, it doesn't. Because memory was not a fact of life before the fall from power we are concerned with."

"You mean there are no memories of that time?"

"Just so."

"This is getting more and more complicated and arduous."

"You thought learning to fly would be easy? Surely not?"

"I thought that there would just be some trick or know-how that you would teach me and then, Bingo, I could fly!"

"Ah, the easy one-step answer that Man is always seeking."

"Maybe I thought there was some essence or medium that would flow from you to me."

"It requires total transformation of Being. Such skills do not come to the powerless, weak and ignorant."

"But it happens sometimes, spontaneous levitation, where even the most inept person finds they have this gift. How do you account for that?"

"A person may take a peep through any door that is left slightly ajar, even if it leads to a room he or she has no right to enter."

This quaint Scots metaphor was a less than satisfactory answer but I realized it was probably all I was going to get.

"I want to know more about the mind. Thought computation and learning has always been considered Man's outstanding advantage over the animals. Now we seem to be dismissing it as a curse, a trivial one at that."

"Trivial, no. But a lower order of function. To think about something is not the same as to experience it. Humans tend to forget that. To 'think about' divine powers is not the same as to experience them; worse, it is to separate yourself from those very things you think about. Do you see that?"

"So what do you think the mind does?"

"First, tell me your understanding."

"Well, the mind is a kind of calculator function. It inputs perceptions of the present to establish the state of the current environment. This is then compared with past experience. The mind then calculates the likely future and chooses the appropriate action to take for the gratification of the organism."

"Bravo. I doubt I could explain it better than that."

"Perhaps then, you can explain for me an awkward paradox?"

"Which is?"

"It is virtually a clichè that we use less than a twentieth of our brain powers. An Indian woman called Shakuntala Devi was able to calculate the 23rd root of a 201 digit number in less time than it took the fastest computer of the day. Compared to that, most of us are dumb mutes at the side of a Shakespearean actor. Why is that?"

"First let me correct the obvious error in this clichè. The brain is not synonymous with mind power. To help, you may be able to tell me evidence for high power metabolism in the brain."

"Well, I do know that approximately a quarter to a third of the body's energy consumption is for the brain. Electrical activity goes on continuously, night and day, in sleep and wakefulness."

"Well then, does this sound like an organ operating at one twentieth of its capacity?"

"Not really!" I replied, chagrined he was giving me a physiology lesson, just to bring me up to speed on the paranormal!

"The reason, Doctor, is very simple: the brain has very little to do with consciousness. It is merely, if you like, a relay from the insubstantial and immanent consciousness to the physical reality. Conscious processes do not take place in the brain…"

"But in the regions around it?"

"Doctor, you would learn faster if you did not interrupt."

"Sorry."

"Consciousness, I keep striving to get across to you, is nothing to do with the physical reality. It is not part of it. It is the *origin*, the source of all there is."

"Reality is only a part of consciousness, right? I'm getting there."

"I think you may be."

"So the mind is not a physical function. But neither is it entirely immaterial?"

"Certainly not. The answer to your paradox is that mind and spirit are misidentified, one with another. They are both of similar order of experience, that is non-physical, and all-pervasive."

"But they are not the same?"

"Not at all."

"What is the point of the mind, then? It seems to be the main stumbling block."

"Indeed, you are right. In an all-knowing condition why would a great godly spirit need such a clumsy contraption as the biological mind? Although it has developed faultlessly it is so subject to error as to be next to worthless for the truth of Being."

"I think the mind does not make mistakes but makes a perfect calculation from the data and experience it is using, like Shakuntala Devi."

"This woman's phenomenal ability is a bad example; do you not understand she made no calculation whatever – she merely *knew* the answer, 'grokked' it, to use your term?"

It was a shocking realization, when it came to me at last. But I still wanted to see the question of mind computation through to the end.

"Only if the mind's input data is faulty or the perception and recall of experience distorted in some detrimental way, then faulty and perhaps destructive thinking is the automatic result."

"I agree. That is why memory is the problem, the whole problem. It is subject to corruption and so valueless as basis for sane judgement."

"Unless there was some way of telling corrupted memory from non-corrupted?"

"Yes, I suppose so."

"Well is there?"

"Not from the point of view of the human mind, no."

I made a decision to spend as long as it takes trying to discover some means by which to distinguish faulty memory from accurate recall.

"Since you have traveled into deep time, Doctor, I would like to explain to you that memories such as you recalled are fraught with dangers."

"Meaning?"

"The universe is a dark and dangerous place. It is filled with things that are best avoided for the moment. But let me just say that long ago there were many powerful beings of evil nature. They decided for their own good, others would be better off as slaves. They had skill, much skill, and mastered a means of trapping unwary beings and subjecting them to overwhelming false memories by which each one was convinced of its own weakness."

"That's how we became weak humans?"

"Only in part. Let us say that the memory entrapment was the mechanism by which free beings allowed themselves to deteriorate. The power of choice was still operative and until the free spirit overthrew itself, there was nothing these Masters of Evil could have done that the Being itself could not have undone."

"All this is terrifying. I'd like to know more."

"In due course."

"But who were these master beings and where did they come from?"

"Let us confine ourselves to your quest."

I think I exhausted him with all those questions! Unfortunately, I had to leave soon after breakfast next day and didn't manage to see him again for several months.

15. Can Physics Help?

I didn't waste my time however. I decided the time was right for a physics showdown with Charles. So I took him for a power lunch, full-on French cuisine, champagne, Meursault and cognac. I wanted him soft and pliable, to bend to my enquiring will!

Still fighting shy of telling him what was going on in my head space, I pressed for ideas and insights from physics on the topic of weightlessness, hoping he wouldn't pay much attention to the similarity in theme to our last encounter.

But he was on it right away.

"Why are you bugged by this weightlessness thing, Doc? You're not thinking of building an antigravity machine?"

"If I am, do you want to help?" I joked.

"No fear. There is one certain way wreck your career in science: to study the five great no-no topics."

"Which are?"

"Free energy from the vacuum, non-Darwinian evolution, cold fusion, antigravity and time travel."

"Well, let's just talk a little about anti-gravity. I'm not thinking about an antigravity machine but human levitation. There are very good accounts of saints levitating; I mean reliable third party accounts. St. Joseph of Cupertino was known to levitate to the height of the pulpit and more during the consecration at the altar. It seems he experienced so many levitations it became necessary to restrict his access to the choir and refectory so as not to cause disturbances during Mass."

"Devoted Catholics would say that was the Holy Spirit visiting."

"Well Catholic saints aren't the only ones; there are lots of those stories, it's true. But oriental mystics are also said to do it—at will. And I have a colleague I trust implicitly who was called to see a patient with a so-called spiritual emergency: she had started levitating and couldn't help herself."

"And you are thinking there must be an explanation at least consistent with modern physics?"

I nodded. This is exactly where I wanted him to pick it up.

"We could start with electro-gravitics."

"What the Hell is that?"

"We skirted on it last time, actually. Sometimes called the Biefield-Brown effect. Biefield was a German; Thomas Townsend Brown was a US scientist. He actually patented his idea in 1928. Basically it was a way of using an electrical field to act on a body in a similar way to gravity, except it could be controlled. Upwards was as good as downwards, so it could make a propulsion system. The US and French governments took it very seriously and researched it for decades. The classified B-2 bomber used depleted uranium on the leading edge of its wing to produce the same effect."

"And you could create this effect in a human?"

"I doubt it; the electrical potential would probably kill them!"

"But birds on high voltage wires don't get electrocuted."

"True. But your human levitator would have to start out in contact with the ground and so would be earthed in the initial conditions. Big flash, gone!"

By this time we had downed the shellfish and a crispy glass or two of wine.

"The thing is, I don't want machines, Charles. Can you come up with something more… natural?"

"We could postulate some kind of standing wave effect that holds a person aloft in an energetic field. Maybe a soliton-like effect."

"Soliton?"

"It's a kind of self-coherent wave. It was first seen in eighteen thirty something by a Scotsman called John Russell. He saw a wave set up by a boat that was very pure and travelled almost indefinitely. He followed it on a horse for miles, without seeing it dissipate. If you could set up a soliton wave of some kind...."

"You mean perpetual motion?"

"Not exactly. But pretty sustained. Solitons occur naturally all the time; like in the tides of the Straits of Gibraltar. Solitons are being studied a lot because they have such fascinating properties. For instance, a soliton wave can overtake and pass another slower wave, passing right through it and emerging at the other side unaltered. In normal dissipating systems the two waves would simply combine."

"OK, what kind of medium would hold a soliton, just water?"

"There's the thing. This is about what we call non-linear waves and there is one fascinating application that we call light bullets. Spheres of light which defy all normal laws of physics. Maybe there is some way a person could get into one of these and be seen to levitate in a field of light."

"Ah, like a saint? I see what you're getting at."

"These are even called halo states," he told me, with a knowing smile.

"It makes me think of a vortex."

"Funny you should say that..."

"Why?"

"Solitons are sometimes accompanied by a chaotic vortex effect. Like the water surging under the stern of a boat when it stops."

"Aren't there supposed to be energy vortices, or vortexes as our American brothers insist on mis-pronouncing it, hidden in the fabric of the universe? Couldn't one of those lead to an anti-gravity effect?"

Charles nodded as he tucked into the Nile perch, which had just arrived. He savoured the sauce to the full and I had to wait over a minute for his next remark.

"I am assuming you don't mean the New Age vortices said to haunt the canyons of the Sedona and the like?" he said at last.

"Well, actually, I have been to Sedona. I definitely felt something at the one they call the Airport Vortex. I felt quite strange; innervated. Maybe I was just happy and clear-headed but it seemed to be more than that. All I can tell you is that I felt an indeterminate but positive sensation there that I hadn't felt before and didn't feel afterwards."

"Well, let's suppose there is something real in Sedona. That could be just a distortion of the Earth's geo-magnetic field. We live in a gigantic force field created by a huge dynamo effect, as the Earth with its iron core rotates in the magnetic field of the Sun. It's billions of gigawatts and more. Even a slight distortion of the field should be significant and detectable, even by a simple biological sensor, such as a human being."

"Well, wouldn't that be enough to charge up a human? Maybe we are back to the electro-gravity effect."

"No, doesn't work," he said dismissively. "There's not enough power to do the work of raising a human body. But let's concentrate on the well-known vortex effect of diminished pressure at the centre. It's called the Bernoulli effect, after the guy who first described it. If you were in a suitable energized medium and that went into the vortex effect, you might get an uplift. That's how a tornado works and snatches things high into the atmosphere."

"It couldn't be air though, otherwise the person would suffocate as the pressure dropped."

"Quite. Also, the spin in air would have to be too fast. It would whip the person off his or her feet. That's not quite levitation, is it?"

Of course, he was right.

"So what kind of energy might do that?"

"Well, suppose it can happen in the zero-point energy field. Maybe that would allow it to impact our space-time reality, instead of just the so-called vacuum."

"Tell me more about zero-point energy." It seemed to me we were struggling for anything to grasp onto that would explain levitation. The zero-point field might be the last shot at a working hypothesis.

"The big buzzword these days," he smiled as he cleared the last of the food from his plate and quaffed it down with yet another mouthful of Meursault. "Zero point is a bit of a misnomer. Even if all mass is removed from the field, a real vacuum in other words, the energy is still present."

"You mean the mass has all transferred to energy?"

"Real particles to virtual particles from the quantum foam, you might say. Look at it another way; if we approach absolute zero—minus two hundred and seventy three degrees on the Kelvin scale—all matter loses energy until it ceases to move. It's absolutely still. Total entropy."

"But nobody has yet reached absolute zero, I know that."

"True. But we've got to within millionths of a degree of the point at which all motion vanishes. Absolute stillness. It's kind of scary because everything in our reality, everything physics stands for, has motion. Time moves, energy moves, stuff is particles that oscillate, wavelengths are all about propagated waves. The whole Cosmos is movement."

By now the Meursault was gone and we were considering a second bottle. Instead, he chose to move on to brandy. The possibility of a dessert was dismissed by a quick wave of the hand.

"You know Charles, this is probably what I was looking for."

"How so?" he asked, understandably puzzled.

"Well, let's take consciousness or the soul, spirit, psyche, whatever you want to call it. All accounts talk about the still point; the calm and total stillness at the center of Being. You know that I define spirit as non-mechanical. So by definition it has no mass, energy, wavelength, no location in space and time, and so on—not unless it considers itself to have location in space and time. But that can be rescinded at will, if only we could remember how to do it!"

He nodded.

"I think the stillness at the point of absolute zero is where the physical universe crosses over to spiritual reality. No motion is the common factor."

"No hope for flying there, Doc," he grinned. "You'd freeze your ass off at absolute zero. Not survivable."

"That's not what I mean. I coming at it from the other end Charles—that if spirit or consciousness can achieve the state of perfect stillness, maybe that's when the mechanical conditions of the physical world cease to operate. A spirit in that state can transcend space, time, gravity, everything we know about the physical world. I think that's why only very holy people seem to be able to levitate, except maybe a few oddballs."

"Well, if that state was real and achievable, it would solve one big problem we have in advanced physics..."

"What's that?"

"We need an observer. There is no such thing as objective reality and truth—because we need an observer to look at all systems. But let's suppose your hypothesis was viable. It would mean we could have an observer from outside the system. That would be cool!" he grinned.

Suddenly, it all came together for me.

"I know all that quantum stuff," I reminded him. "About collapsing the wave function and choosing reality; it needs an observer to do that. There is no reality without an observer, that's the Copenhagen interpretation, after Neils Bohr, right?"

He nodded assent.

"I read a few years ago about some physics professor guy trying to derive new quantum equations that actually take account of consciousness. It's like we have to have consciousness to have any reality at all. The idea of an independent universe seems doomed to fail by the very nature of things."

"Actually, I can take it a step further, Doc," he announced. "It's not just conscious awareness. At the deepest level, physics is about language. I'll accept that language is a hallmark of consciousness. It's an information universe. By information, I mean that consciousness is implied. But that's my point. Consciousness rules, at some deeper fundamental level we don't yet understand."

"Well then, why can't we just click our fingers and some object materializes? Why can't we fly without wings, just postulating the ability to rise up and travel wherever we wish. If it comes to that, why travel at all? Just BE someplace else."

"Well, there are sporadic accounts of all these phenomena, as you know Doc. So I think the question you are really asking is why can't we all do it, any time we choose?"

"I suppose I am..."

"I think it comes back to language. What words we have shape our reality.

He was getting animated and it was not just the alcohol speaking. I could see some hidden passion flowing to the surface. Charles loved talking at this level. That's why I took him to lunch on a regular basis!

"The important thing, Doc, is that you need to see physics in the right way. It's not, as people think, an advanced explanation of the world. It's just a language. A way of describing the world we see, or think we see."

"What do you mean?"

"There is a sense in which no-one, including the philosophers, doubts the existence of a real objective world. That's what we experience every day. But when we come to talk about it, everything transforms into some other world, a layer of reality which is delimited by what we think and the terms we use, not by what is."

"Are you saying magic is just another language?"

"That's exactly what I am saying. The alchemists of old were probably doing stuff that we could only dream of, at least until radio-activity came along, when we started to understand the natural transmutation of base substances. But maybe they could do it, because they had a different model universe, compounded by a different language that gave them a whole different experience."

"I see what you mean. So we can dismiss them today as fools or charlatans because we've altered their language?"

"Take electrons. When we talk about electrons, people think of them as perfectly respectable bits of matter—real, in other words. But we now know they are the darndest things to catch in words. An electron is a wave, a particle, a nothing, a something. They are supposed to just leap out of the zero point energy field—each one alongside a positron, to balance the books nicely—and then both disappear again, just as magically as they appeared. It's Alice In Wonderland stuff."

"You couldn't make this stuff up, as they say."

"Well, quite. What it comes down to is that what you have words for is what you find! Physicists have certain words for things they see and talk about; leptons, quarks, things like that. That creates their understanding of reality. Mathematicians are a different bunch and they see reality in a different way, another abstract language. And here let me tell you a big secret to this universe..."

His voice dropped to a whisper and I found myself leaning forward, to listen like a conspirator.

"There is nothing whatever that connects math with the real world. It's one of the biggest illusions of all time. We find that certain figures will make predictions about reality. But when it comes down to it, the predicted effects are only more numbers."

"Like Einstein's predictions of the 1918 eclipse and the photographs taken in Principe?"

"Exactly. Einstein's predictions were very accurate. But only in predicting more numbers..."

"Like the amount of bend in a ray of starlight! The amount of the effect was just another number," I came in excitedly, grasping where he was going with this surprise twist.

"I mean, what the hell does three mean? What is that?" Charles held up three fingers, waving them a little wildly. "It's not a number, it's a word! We've got finger-finger-finger but three is just a word, a concept, not a reality. Take away the word and there is no reality; we're back to finger-finger-finger. Think about it."

The waiter arrived with the bill but I ignored it, as the conversation was getting fascinating.

"The lesson is that what we are comfortable talking about and the language we regularly use creates for us a sense of what is real," Charles continued, after I rejected his gestures of paying for his meal.

I pondered this for some time. If Charles was correct, I was starting to enter the fairy reality, because that was becoming for me a language describing the new reality the fairy was trying to introduce me to.

"So you are saying there is no right way to describe the world. No *true* reality, that merits special descriptive terms, above other ways of looking and seeing? Just different languages?"

"That's exactly what I'm saying," he smiled.

"So, directly or indirectly, you think that consciousness is the originator of reality?"

"It's a given. And remember this, Doc: that nothing is so weird and woo-woo—including life after death, magical flying or reverse travel through time—that advanced physics says it can't happen. In fact, advanced physics predicts that most of these strange New Age ideas not only could happen—but *must happen!* It's an information and energy universe, not a mechanical one!"

Well, he'd earned his lunch OK!

So really science agrees with what the fairy has said all along. Only our blind acceptance of so-called "laws" prevents us breaking them. Shift your conscious world-view and you shift reality. And flying would not occur only in my mind, as I feared, but in the new universe that I create in place of the old, tired one!

There was no conflict with outlandish physics theories. But since I had first appealed to the Fairy, who had agreed to help, I decided it was only sensible to follow his path and not expect Charles to come up with the answers.

I was ready to meet with my magical mentor, for the next step of the journey.

That night, I fell asleep with the words of T S Eliot in my heart and mind, from *Burnt Norton*, the first of his "Four Quartets":

At the still point of the turning world. Neither flesh nor fleshless;
Neither from nor towards; at the still point, there the dance is,
But neither arrest nor movement. And do not call it fixity,
Where past and future are gathered. Neither movement from nor towards,
Neither ascent nor decline. Except for the point, the still point,
There would be no dance, and there is only the dance.
I can only say, there we have been: but I cannot say where.

For The Reader:

You have to try this, even if it is one of the hardest meditations of all: sit or lie, relax, get into alpha and try to slow down everything you experience. *Everything,* from breathing, thinking, heartbeat, energy and Being. Go in, in and in, until you find peace and calm. Then go further, much further; look for the stillness, the awesome stillness at your Being's core. If you find it any time in your lifetime, you've done well!

16. The Fall from Grace

It was several more weeks before I got away from work again and drove all night, to maximize my time on Skye. The next encounter did not go at all the way I expected.

In fact things took a remarkable turn when I went to look for him along the cliff tops of Dunvegan Head. Instead of his familiar form, I was astonished to see a female figure coming towards me. She too wore a cloak, dyed with the soft red of crotal, a lichen which grows in the Isles. She was far younger and fairer in countenance than the figure of the grumpy male fairy.

"I was expecting someone else," I said nervously. "Or perhaps you are that same person in a different form?"

The question sounded silly.

"The being you met was one who you would probably call my father."

"But he isn't really?"

"Hardly, in truth. We are both immortal. We have always lived and always will. That makes me as old as he is!"

"From what I learned yesterday, I am every bit as old as you both."

"Doctor, you are learning fast!"

"I am glad to talk with someone new. Your father must have grown weary of my questions and demands."

"On the contrary, he told me you were very receptive and interesting to talk to."

"So what shall we talk about?"

"My father, thought you might appreciate a history lesson."

"History? That seems strange, when he has been trying to convince me that time has no meaning. What is history without time?"

"Real history is beyond time. It is a sacred composition of all realities to which one is heir. He thought you might like to hear a little about the progress of spirit in this sector of the conjoint universe."

"Try me."

"Actually, progression is a poor word. It seems a regression, really."

"How do you mean?"

"Long ages ago, those we now call human spirits were powerful gods and goddesses. In this condition, a spirit would have no definite attachment to a body. In other words, the being could exercise consciousness without the need of physical senses and the dynamics of interaction with material substances."

"In other words, we *thought* it and it happened."

"Nowadays you would call it magic. But we are talking no more than the properties of a conscious entity which controls creation - indeed which made creation, long long ago. It might be interesting for you to speculate with me, how such an all-powerful being could become weakened by its own ideas and trapped by its own actions, so as to lose its limitless powers and freedom."

"Hold on, I want to make some notes here."

"You will remember everything I say, I promise you. You will be able to write up your notes at home in the evening."

It would take real magic to be able to fix this for me; my memory hasn't been that great of late! Yet she was right.

"At the beginning, as you might say, before there was Time or any such concept as beginning, *Causal Consciousness* was simply a quality of Being. Creation was a spiritual state of energy, not a physical reality as you know it today."

This sounded somewhat like the Vedic state of Brahmin or the *ground*, an all-pervasive matrix. I was fascinated.

"Individual consciousness would be local accretions of this energy within the universal ground. For this to happen, there *has to be a degree of separation*."

"But there is basic oneness, as many people believe?"

"There is much nonsense talked about "oneness". All one is a contradiction in terms."

"An oxymoron? How so?"

"We are either just-one, in which case we as individual entities do not exist, or separated, as implied by the plural term *all*. The absurdity of the former is evident from the moment you open your eyes every morning. What is important, of course, is that we all come from the same place. In this I include the Old People and others like us. We are of the same order and category of stuff, or I should say none-stuff, as you! We share things and have common needs and reality at this time."

"But you are saying we are not all-as-one, the moment we recognize our individuality?"

"Exactly. From this argument follows the state we may call Free Being. The basic rule seemed to be that consciousness experienced whatever it considered it wanted to experience. The "rules" of reality could be made and unmade at will; universes created and uncreated; viewpoints made and unmade arbitrarily; in short there were no barriers, beyond those that were purposely created."

"Yes, I had a glimpse of this time. Flying, and I suppose dematerializing, were entirely natural and to be expected at such an epoch?"

"Of course."

"So when and why did it start to change for us; for us who became humans, at least?"

"In the long ages of time, a Being in this state will need to invent games."

"Zeus!"

"Doctor, do I have a problem, or would others find it equally hard to understand what you just said?" She was smiling but not mocking.

"I meant the Greek gods; Zeus and the lesser gods. They were always playing games, some of which were very bad news for humans. According to legend, anyway."

"Well, at first the games can be made and played by self. But that has only limited excitement and validity, like playing yourself at chess; not very challenging. Eventually, one would need other viewpoints, which are either found or made, something with which to compete."

"Made? Do you mean that consciousness can fracture and multiply, like organisms dividing?"

"Absolutely. Some creations of the primordial consciousness would appear separate, because the spirit forgot – or chose not to remember - that it had made them and endowed these newer entities with life. Remember the rule: anything can happen that consciousness considers can happen."

"But that's anarchy."

"Of a kind."

"So already one must introduce the concept of a Higher Order, some purpose, or some controlling force that regulates the universe?"

"Has it not always been so? In this case the time-word "always" means simply that it was never not-so."

"So we are discussing, really, how and why the universe and multiple consciousness came into being!"

"Very good, Doctor. My father said you were most stimulating."

"Not really, I just enjoy being taught these things."

"This is not teaching, Doctor. Say only that the sharing of love and knowledge is rather like taking a journey together."

When I thought about this, it was true. I didn't feel I was being pumped full of data. I felt it was an evolution of thought and I was participating in it.

"For the first time, the Free Being began to contact other Free Beings. From then on it is not a unique universe but must be, by definition, a shared experience. Certain rules would need to be in place, in order to define what we mean by agreement. Otherwise it would indeed be very chaotic."

"But fairies don't always play by the rules. They get to seem powerful!"

"Remember every game is played at the level you agree to. You made these agreements with us long ago and then forgot you made them!"

"If you say so."

"Spontaneous interchange of ideas, energy, particles and emotion with other Beings is the basis for a very pleasant existence. Paradise, as it is usually conceived as a religious enticement, would belong at this level."

"So, what went wrong?"

"Unfortunately, over time and, as games became more complicated in order to keep them stimulating, mistakes would lead to *infringement.* The basic definition of infringement is interfering with other peoples' purposes, matter and energy in space and time which we do not own."

"And this would include the frustration of desires, as much as the enforcement of unwanted outcomes? Stopping something desirable would be as much an infringement as doing something undesirable." I could see that, without her needing to say yes.

"In the beginning, infringement would be no more than unintentional displacement of another's interests and probably not very serious in degree. In the nature of reality, it is hardly possible to conceive independent goals and purposes, without there being an element of conflict or obstruction to somebody, somewhere."

"That's what makes a game a game, right? But we still agreed to the games... We exposed ourselves deliberately to hurt?"

She nodded assent.

At this point we reached the headland and chose to descend and sit on the rocky shore. The rumble and rush of the sea seemed to take on a new voice, that spoke of the rhythms of the universe, as much as the heartbeat of the world's oceans.

"Nevertheless," she continued, "It was an amiable and not too stressful emergence, which would probably add spice and purpose to existence."

"Rather like a cricket match: there would be plenty of thrust and counter-effort as part of the excitement—but a losing player would not wish to call in the police because a bowler had successfully knocked over his wicket!"

"A very good metaphor."

"So how did it ultimately become destructive?"

"More serious is the matter of transgression. Here things have degenerated to the intentional, or at least willing acceptance, that another is going to be compromised, disadvantaged or hurt. In the excitement of cut and trust, we cut a corner or break a rule, to be sure of our triumph. We have progressed now to the matter of a *spiritual crime*— doing wrong. It is not a moral or legal matter but a judgement of the heart: something you should not have done! It makes no matter how much the being or person dresses it up with excuses; at bottom, he or she knows it was wrong."

"But one always knows when one has transgressed. It hurts us! We feel uncomfortable."

"Indeed. There is spiritual pain and a certain amount of decay. For you have fallen away a little from the true nature of your Being. And that is the problem: from here on down it starts to go from bad to worse. The Free Being has surrendered a certain quality of independence and is on the way to becoming trapped, limited and weak. The next part of the mechanism sees to that."

"Which is?"

"Once the being has transgressed and experienced the negative pain and loss of status, it becomes careful. There is an attempt to avoid such self-damage by avoiding doing anything at all. This state of holding back on causation is what fundamentally weakens the being. He or she is now no longer a god or goddess; no longer perfect. Gradually, as mistakes and transgressions begin to pile up, more and more power is surrendered until, in time, power and high-level insight, any divine ability, is seen as a negative, something to be avoided because it will lead to trouble!"

"I begin to see why, in most human societies, anyone who stands out as having special magical or divine powers is singled out for ferocious attack."

"Is this not what happened to the one you call Christ?"

"Well then, why not Buddha?"

"The Christ laid claim to being divine but that humans were not and could never be. Buddha, on the other hand, made it plain that, in his own view, he was not divine – or rather that we all were."

"Then isn't the obsession with an alien "One-God" in truth just a means of keeping clear of the matter of our own inherent god-like qualities? Certainly one way to avoid the uncomfortable knowledge that we all had the powers you describe is to pretend they are uniquely enshrined in an unusual being, which is a remote entity and unlike the rest of us! Yet we imbue it with attitudes just like our own..."

"Exactly, Doctor. And isn't this what we see? The supposed One-God is inhered with our problems, attitudes and mistakes. He, or She, is made vengeful and arbitrary; almost petulant in demanding favors and honor. That does not fit the logical definition of a true god."

She left me a few moments to think about this.

"So what happens next in this slow decline?" seemed the obvious question.

"Now, sadly, this weakened being has become *effect*; where once it held sway over all matter, energy, space and time under its perception, it is now helpless. It has retreated and surrendered all powers, due to trying to avoid hurtful mistakes and infringements on others."

"So this is the point where evil beings were able to take control and blank out the soul's memory of the deep distant past when it was free?"

"Such a blow could only have been possible consequent on a decision by the being, which effectively allows such an invasion."

"So we had to empower the enemy!"

"Correct. Now the Once-Free Being thinks it has to "obey" matter, energy, space and time. Since everything that happens is beyond one's control there is little to do but worry."

"Now I understand Man's chronic anxiety! This all-too-human condition is basically that of being effect and with no real options to control one's future or environment. No wonder there is tension and fear on the streets."

"Below worry is guilt. If you have ever been there, you will know how incapacitating and destructive this feeling is: all the misery of being to blame but none of the benefits, such as freedom and self-worth."

"That's true. As a doctor, I have naturally studied some psychology. I know that if you want to stop someone doing something to you, or something you don't like, try to make them feel guilty for it. It's a poor control mechanism, as countless humans have found in their scrabbling around for tricks or mechanisms to get back some degree of control over their lives. But those who use it are easily subject to the same trap themselves. So where do we go from here?"

"We have now created the universe to which you and every other human being subscribes, believing that you must. A world where you do not control reality, a solid fixed world that is alien, inanimate and invested with forces that will kill you if try to violate its precepts. Not a very happy place to be!"

"Is there any way to escape the trap we have created for ourselves? Say there is, please! There are many stories of fairies turning into mortals, can we be promoted in the opposite direction and turn into fairies, or even gods again?"

Once more, the question sounded very silly but you would want to ask it too, if you were in my place.

"Of course," she replied.

"How?"

"By following the path to truth."

"That sounds slightly glib. Religions have been saying that since the dawn of time; each one then claims a monopoly on what that truth is."

"Remember, this fall is a being on the way down. On the way up, it reverses. It means taking responsibility for all that one has done, unconditionally. The way back up this ladder is a matter of confronting and redeeming what we have done to ourselves and others. This is a personal truth. It is a long hard road and a matter of the utmost urgency, since the window of escape here on Earth is diminishing fast and may soon be closed."

"You make it sound very scary. Why should Earth be coming to an end?"

"Earth has a special place in this phase of conscious evolution that you simply do not understand. It would be a shame to see the door to ascension closed on the few who wish it, because of the folly and crimes of those who do not understand."

She would not elaborate on this final remark, no matter how much I pressed her.

"Confronting evil is also the royal highway to happiness. There can be no bliss or joy below the level of transgression. Once enveloped in the turmoil and grime of committing bad acts against our fellow creatures, intentionally or heedlessly, we are creating our own hell from which there can be no escape, other than ceasing such acts and getting clean of their taint."

"Like saints?"

"It is not for nothing, Doctor, that the light of joy and divine powers should be associated with those who lead saintly and beneficient lives, helping and easing the pain of others. Knowingly or unknowingly, they have discovered the simple spiritual truth that *bad acts harm one*."

"Many saints or holy men and women were reputedly fliers. St Agnes of Montepulciano and St Catherine of Siena, to mention two, and of course Asian saints, such as Nagendra nath Bhaduri. Are you saying if I become like them, I shall be able to fly?"

"You will have access to energies not presently recognized by science. What you do with them will be your choice."

"I'll take that as a yes. Then how does one become a saint? It seems they are born not made."

"Not so. Many were notorious sinners who became won over to higher ideals."

"But how can we consciously make this transition?"

"The answer lies in atonement."

"Tell me the way."

"Doctor, I believe you already have great insight into the answer."

"I'm not sure. But a lot of ideas are coming fast. For example, confession makes a person feel lighter. Wrong-doing is the opposite; we speak of a heavy conscience; being burdened by guilt; weighed down. When atoned we are clear and light-hearted, as we say. It all makes sense to me now."

"Oh Doctor, the tide is about our ankles and you haven't noticed. That is enough for today, I think. When next you meet my father, he will explain the way forward. He was touched by your openness and desire to learn."

"I have one last question," I said, as we rose to begin our walk back.

"Go on."

"If we restore our spiritual abilities and become once more powerful, free, loving and wise, what is to *stop us deteriorating again?* You can't just say we will be back to wisdom and would be knowing enough to avoid trouble. We were wise once and yet allowed ourselves to decay in endless spirals through time, clearly. We were gods or god-like and now we are human. How can we believe that wisdom, power and love will protect us when it didn't in the past?"

"A most insightful point, Doctor. The final answer must come from forces of enlightenment greater than any of us, free beings or human saints. Our task, the Old People believe, is simply to do our best and shine the beauty of love and truth upon all things."

And with that, she was gone.

For the reader:

I found the following exercise very useful at this point. It could be called a walk for atonement.

In a time when time is your own, undertake a walk of at least one mile. Walk slowly and at every step, make a pronouncement of love and forgiving:

> I forgive myself
> I forgive all others
> I forgive myself for my sins

I forgive [...name...] for what he/she did
I forgive myself for my errors
I forgive [...others...] for what he/she did
I have trapped others into transgressing against me. I forgive them and accept my responsibility

In truth you can compose and vary these statements as you walk. You know who are the people you complain about in life and those who feel wronged by you. Over a typical mile you will voice your love and forgiveness over 2,000 times!

This is a kind of meditation. You could do it sitting down. But the rhythm of gently walking gives the procedure an almost hypnotic quality, which adds power. Moreover, making the effort raises you to more commitment. Think about the words. If you don't like words, just parade the notion. But you must be involved and not merely chanting words (as with rote prayers).

Notice, as you atone, you feel lighter; more ready to fly!

17. The Freedom to Fly

Next morning, I awoke to find myself flying. My body floated off the floor and slowly drifted upwards and forwards. I wasn't going through any conscious process; it just happened. I wanted to try and turn over, face downwards, but nothing I thought had any effect.

It occurred to me that I was probably afraid that the flying would come to a sudden end and that would mean crashing to the floor on my face. It was that Judas fear again. How much it haunts the vaults of our consciousness, destroying our hopes, opportunities and dreams.

So I tried to go backwards. I thought "backwards", grunted with effort and even said out loud "go back" but to no avail. I realized that was silly. Effort or force could have no part in the achievement of flying, only decision and power.

Slowly, without my being able to do anything, my body drifted back to the ground. The whole experience had not been more than about 90 seconds, I suppose.

But I had done it! It had started!

I was exulted and gulped down breakfast. Dashing out of the hotel, I felt as light as a feather, free as a bird.

It never occurred to me that I had hallucinated in the semi-waking state, or that perhaps I had concentrated so intensely on the problem for so long, keeping my mind at fever pitch, that I had begun to imagine responses.

My mentor was not impressed and dismissed it at once and wanted to get down to work. Apparently he didn't really believe I had flown at all. But the strange feeling I had lasted more than a day. I felt as if I were new made and like a child in heaven. All the colours were intense and bright; objects seemed to have special reverence; and people were all my loving friends.

But since the fairy didn't think much of my achievement, I seemed foolish to protest and so I just got down to work.

"Come, my ardent young friend. Tell me what you have learned since last we spoke." I noticed the word "friend" and was flattered by this exaltation.

"I was talking with your daughter about our state of spiritual evolution here on Earth. I seem to have understood that cleansing and atonement is central to success in developing renewed states of consciousness. She made it clear I needed to know much more about cleaning up my failed and dirty past, which would otherwise inhibit my move towards freedom and enlightenment."

"It is an old ritual Doctor, for all those who seek enlightenment and peace."

"But do I have to uncover and atone for all those things I did throughout eternity?"

"Fortunately, no. To master the principle is sufficient, though in itself no small undertaking. Your time line goes back a very long way, as I have demonstrated to you, and there may be very dark sinister material deep in the past, so long ago you would scarcely remember it. But by inference you may thus correct your side-spin and get back into the center position, of goodness and decency in thought, word and deed. The sickness of past behaviors will then drop away and become unimportant."

"But I would still have to face up to and take the burden of huge numbers of wicked deeds?"

"More than the average human could stomach, I'm afraid."

"If you will, I would like to ask you to talk more on this theme. It both fascinates and appals me, it's implications. You seem to be saying that unless one keeps one's consciousness bright and clean, that it is not possible to fly?"

"Indeed not, Doctor. To fly requires a considerable change and adaptation of consciousness, as I have been trying to tell you. This can hardly take place if the consciousness instrument itself is clogged and malfunctioning."

"So, like a car cannot travel quickly or be economical if its points and plugs are dirty, you are saying?"

"That is not my language Doctor. But I do understand your analogy and I would say yes, in principle."

"So, in a way, to be able to fly is a test of moral and ethical integrity, as well as mastering a strange skill from deep within the mind?"

"That is so."

"You'd better tell me more," I said, with a barely disguised sigh. I'm sure he noticed it, anyway.

"All humans are doing the same thing, essentially: trying to do right."

"Even Hitler, Pohl Pot, Charles Manson?" I slipped into the cheap cliché without wishing to. I wondered what his answer was. But I already knew…

"Even these evil men did not consider their acts were wrong; perhaps wrong for others but not wrong for them."

"I tend to agree. In my researches I have become more and more convinced that the human psyche is not consciously able to commit evil. It's a religious myth. A person cannot act against their basic belief that what they do and think is right. So even if we think of an act as blatantly evil and wrong, the individual committing such an act does not."

"Very good, Doctor. Please continue…"

"Well, as I see it, we may know that others regard a certain action as a sin, whatever—we have been told and acknowledge that we have been told so. We may even admit that we ourselves regard it as bad—some of the time. But at the precise moment of committing as a sin, we think it is acceptable.

We invent plausible reasons why this time the action is different from all other times."

"Wisely put, Doctor. Now there is a condition of change which we know as *transgression* or causing harm. Betrayal is beyond this and enters into malevolent and corrupted evil intent. But even a traitor has supposed that his wicked deed is justifiable; he or she will have some valid excuse. The Quisling is no more wicked than the rest of humankind; just stupid and misguided. Transgression on the other hand is a common experience; we enter it often in a mild degree — best called infringement — in day-to-day relations with our people. For some, sadly, it becomes a way of life. Married couples often live in endless strife, which is this state of play magnified and continued, because neither has the courage or integrity to put a stop to it."

"I suppose we recognize this as getting into "games" with family, friends, customers or other life relations with the intent of "teaching them a lesson". Revenge, spite or any of these all-too-common emotions of ill will is just a state of constant transgression."

"Exactly."

"So basically, transgression means doing damage, committing harm, even if there was no original intention to do so?"

"I am not talking here about making a mistake or accidentally doing something which causes a problem. Most decent people would simply own up, put it right and get on with their lives. Mistakes, as you know, are unfortunate but not evil. I am talking instead about a persistent or recurring state. It persists because the individual defends it. To recognize and correct a state of transgression requires a high degree of integrity and resolve. It may not be easy, especially if the harm has gone on for some time."

"But a transgression need not only be an act of commission?"

"No, to *fail to do something within our power* which would lessen another's hurt or injury is just as much an act of spiritually degrading vandalism as to do something destructive to them."

"Ah, Jeremy Bentham." I expected he knew who the philosopher Jeremy Bentham was. In any case, if he didn't, he seemed not to bother to find out.

This was not the first time I wondered if a fairy had encyclopaedic knowledge, or just deep wisdom, not based on our kind of learning at all. I made a note to ask him some time later whether knowing all about everything meant one would have pat the dates of the kings and queens or chemical formulas or know how to solve complex mathematical riddles?

"We all desire to exist in harmony," he continued. "Side by side, each of us wants to live our life and we expect, hope and desire that no-one will interfere with us or spoil our dreams, plans and manoeuvres. For that brings unhappiness. Being thwarted—loss, failure or being stopped—is the basis of almost all psychological ills. As an aside, Doctor, I offer this as a clean new definition of stress."

"Makes a lot of sense."

"Each individual being has his or her own boundaries; territory or space which represents "us", as distinct from anyone else or any other territory."

"But, aside from the obvious state of madness, why would anyone cross these boundaries and create strife?"

"Quite simply, others have their own plans and desires too. Sometimes purposes and actions clash in opposition to each other, without harmful intention. Inevitably, in the random melee of life, with its infinitely complex and varied dance of individual lives and dramas, paths cross and intertwine in ways which interfere, one with another. This is a function of social complexity probably. The more dense society and the movement that goes on within it, the more inevitable and frequent these clashes of purpose will be. It is almost impossible to follow down each thread of consequence and to see the full ramifications of a given course of behavior."

"So the randomness turns into strife, almost unintentionally?"

"Quite so."

"Most of us desire to do good and despair of our accursed actions that bring harm to self and others. I ask you humbly, what do we do about this condition? Is there a step-by-step plan for freeing one's self from harmful conflicts?"

"The first step is simply recognizing one has done wrong and owning up to it. No lightweight feat for many, it seems."

"Owning up is often the hardest part!"

"This means, I must stress, being able to state it to the party one has harmed. Without this candid acceptance of responsibility, the rest avails nothing. Next comes the decisive elimination of whatever quirk, trait, attitude, falsehood or personal weakness caused the trespass in the first place. Get rid of it, totally and forever."

"This may require a considerable degree of self-awareness and psychological insight."

"I did not say it was easy. In fact, it is one of the hardest adjustments of Being that humans need to make. Identifying what it was that drove us to iniquitous behaviour is naturally a most important preliminary to correcting it. One must also be willing to eradicate even the tendency to behave prejudicially to others. That is fundamental to ethical and sociable living."

I could see that many people were not going to succeed at this step but that unless it is carried out thoroughly and conscientiously, the situation will simply keep recurring. Courage, honesty and shouldering blame for one's own acts are the key here.

"Next comes the stage of making up the damage that one has caused. Without a willingness to put right whatever harm has accrued to others (and to self) by one's transgressions, there is no real liberation, healing or recovery."

"This is probably the true meaning of atonement as I understand the term, and is the true burden of responsibility."

"Yet if the first two steps are done correctly, the individual should then feel *impelled to put matters to rights*. In this step mere apologizing is not enough. Admitting one is in the wrong is not enough. There have been losses and damage. This must be amended for the deed to be cleansed. Making up for the damage is something a person *feels*, not merely a state or time interlude. It is done when it is done, and not before. He or she *knows* they are now clean on the issue."

"So the end of atonement is not contrition but a certain feeling that betokens the return of happiness and self-respect?"

"More than that even; it heralds a return to power and grace. This is where you will find your first experience of lightness and levity. The important *therapeutic* nature of atonement needs to be emphasized. The healing and relief comes alike to the victim and the perpetrator. A simple act of forgiveness will release the victim. But this is not enough for the malefactor. Only full atonement will do that, for which the reward is a considerable recovery of missing spiritual powers. One allows one's self to regain some of the god or goddess status, because one has taken responsibility for harm caused in the past and restored good to its place. This means we need no longer be fearful of the accidental and destructive consequence of our powers."

"Does it mean that it is harmful to an oppressor or transgressor to forgive them without any attempts at atonement in view?"

"Rightly, it is not within our power to truly forgive someone who knows that the taint lingers and is sickened by it. The *apparency* of "getting away with it" is just that—a complete illusion. It isn't smart to think that just because life hasn't punished us that nothing will come of it. We will bring retribution on ourselves in some form or other."

"The corollary then, is that we should strive to clean up our misdeeds and keep a shine on our conscience?"

"Without atonement and the re-assertion of causality and therefore responsibility, one remains forever weakened and irresponsible, a victim of one's own crimes. This is how great beings become weakened and lose their inherent divinity."

"I see."

"There was an old and revered tradition in English culture that one played "cricket". In this sense the sporting connection was merely metaphorical, meaning one took care of the ripples that one made in life. You did not "put one over" on another person and expect to get away with it."

"Does this mean that the actual degree or severity of consequences is not relevant to whether the state exists or not; merely how important it is and how pressing the need to correct it?"

"Correct. Minor infringements can usually be cleared up in moments, with no more than a word of love and apology. Some misdeeds could take literally years to properly atone for. If you borrow a friend's car without asking, that is a clear transgression. If you crash it while uninsured, that is worse. If you took people for a joy ride and someone was killed, that would be a pretty horrible degree."

"But the same quality of relationship exists if you merely borrow a book and spill coffee on it. To correct the imbalance of the latter may only require you buy a new book or substitute it with something else?"

"Just so."

"It's a tough philosophy and these days everyone is looking for the instant quick fix!"

"Yes, it can be very tough entering the zone of atonement. It can be a personal living hell. But there is a simple rule which will comfort and encourage you to do right, Doctor."

"Which is?"

"The harder it is to admit one has behaved badly and transgressed against another, the bigger the damaging effect that act is having on your own psyche."

"So if it were a trivial matter, it would be easy to own up and get on with life. But the fact that we find the barrier of effort is very great, means we must also know, deep down inside, that what we did was pretty wicked and impossible to defend. That's why we bounce off and want to stay clear."

"You should not give up your day job, Doctor, but you do sometimes have a happy turn of phrase, yes indeed!"

"This is so different from the principle of religious penitence. So much more enlightened. Penitence smacks too much of punishment. Official revenge and reprisal degrade the authority that imposes them; many men and women have seen that. It also implies lack of an adequate philosophy and any practical solution to behavioral problems."

"Punishment is not healing. Self-acknowledgement and taking responsibility are the keys to recovery. The inadequacy of punishment and reprisal is part of a wider law that says that no-one can accept the truth on another's behalf. It has to be discovered for ourselves."

"Of course."

"I see now. So the religious philosophy of a 'redeemer' is meaningless, set against the great laws of the universe?"

"Redemption is a very personal matter, as is enlightenment."

"Does this not then lead to the Buddhist law of Karma which states, simply, what you give out will return to influence you equally. The Christian Bible also has a maxim "As ye sow, so shall ye reap" which means much the same thing."

"These are different statements of the universal law, that you cannot harm another without also harming yourself in turn. Behaving wickedly will lead to a collapse of spiritual powers."

There is no avoiding this universal sanction, which is as inescapable as Newton's Third Law: *action and reaction are equal and opposite.* A force pushing on something kicks back on the pusher just as hard.

"So the idea of a wicked, powerful monster, a black sorcerer, for example, is just a myth. Evil cannot spawn spiritual powers?"

"Not quite so simple, dear Doctor. But let's leave it at that for the moment."

"Well answer me this: there are many ordinary and by no means well behaved people who have claimed to fly. Does this mean they are lying?"

"No. But there is a difference between it happening by chance and being able to control it at will. I presume, Doctor, that you did not merely want to wake up one morning with the ceiling a few inches from your nose!"

Ouch! He got me.

For the reader:

It might be smart to spend some time writing down one's known transgressions. If you have done something you know you should not have, you need to clean this up, for your own sake. Then take them up with the individuals concerned, using this simple (but tough!) 5-stage plan:

As the fairy explained, there are four clearly identifiable steps to clearing culpable trespass against others:

1. **Admission**

   Recognizing and being willing to state plainly that one has done wrong and harmed another is essential. Without this degree of honesty, the rest avails nothing. Fudging, evasion, justifications, excuses, blaming others, and so forth, have no place in the candid acceptance of responsibility that is required in step 1.

2. **Identifying The Cause Of Corruption.**

   It is vital to deal decisively with whatever quirk, trait, attitude, misundertanding, falsehood etc caused the trespass in the first place. Get rid of it, totally and forever. This may require a considerable degree of self-awareness and psychological insight. If you are stuck, consult some popular texts elaborating the theme that we create our own adversity.

3. **Correcting The Damage Which Ensued.**

   Next comes the stage of making up the damage that one has caused. Without a willingness to put right whatever harm has accrued to others (and to self) by one's transgressions, there is no real liberation, healing or recovery.

4. **Asking Forgiveness**

   Finally, and ONLY after 1,2 and 3, comes the act of contrition and the humble submission for forgiveness and re-acceptance.

Creating A Better Version Of Events

The final stage, he told me, was to recreate the memory of past events in a more empowering way. I protested that facts were facts and couldn't be changed. He dismissed my idea as human conceit: that our memory should be the one which defines truth was just arrogant folly.

Do this in a relaxed time, with your eyes closed, and really visualize how it could have been better. You'll soon find it easy to alter the past and your reaction to it.

Just create a full substitute "memory" that is glorious and empowering to you, free of the hurts and bad behavior. I promise you this is just as capable of influencing your thoughts and feelings as a "real" memory.

18. Was I talking To Myself?

The next day was the last on this trip. My mind was jammed to capacity with so many overwhelming new ideas, all of which needed a lot of thinking about. I decided to keep this final day for myself and take a long walk. There was one place on Skye where I knew I could find the kind of solitude I was looking for, another place called Boreraig but fifty miles away at the opposite end of the island, on the shores of Loch Eishort.

It is an arduous three-hour walk from the little ruined church of *Chille Chriosd* in Strath Suardal, where I parked my car.

This beautiful grassy sward had once sheltered a small township, home to over a hundred souls. But in the late nineteenth century, when times were hard, the settlement had been abandoned. One day a boat for the Americas had sailed into the bay and virtually the entire population had given up their subsistence struggle here and embarked for a new life.

Since then, Boreraig has been deserted, the houses now lay all about in ruins but the outlines remain visible, the streets and walkways quite clear. There are no roads to the bay and few people ever come near today. Only the roar of the sea, the constant wind and the plaintive mewing of sea birds disturb this lonely vale.

And the memories. The past clings here. It is a haunted place, redolent with the presence of generations past. It was as if everyone was still here, just the other side of a curtain hanging there…

I was reminded of Chief Seattle and a famous speech attributed to him: "*And when the last Red Man shall have perished, and the memory of my tribe shall have become a myth among the White Men, these shores will swarm with the invisible dead of my tribe, and when your children's children think themselves alone in the field, the store, the shop, upon the highway, or in the silence of the pathless woods, they will not be alone. In all the earth there is no place dedicated to solitude. At night when the streets of your cities and villages are silent and you think them deserted, they will throng with the returning hosts that once filled them and still love this beautiful land.*"

I sat under the shelter of an old mountain ash or rowan tree, growing through the tumbled walls of one of the former homes. The sun shone, the sea looked positively Mediterranean and benevolence lingered in the air. The grass here was greener than other parts of the island and there were patches of intense yellow-green where the curd residues from emptied butter churns had fertilized the soil. Man's crude hand, I thought, is not always destructive!

I reflected on all that I had learned.

Sometimes it pays to use the Eastern way and not tackle the problem head on. A result can be obtained obliquely, sneaking up on the truth from behind, if you like a playful metaphor. To want to fly is just another craven desire, a need – perhaps no purer than addiction to alcohol or tobacco. To grasp and desire so ardently could be a weakness.

The way I would solve this problem, I decided, was by the pursuit of knowledge for its own sake. The fairy had said as much – that learning to fly was a voyage of self-discovery, a conquest of the inner domain of me, not an overthrow of the laws of physics! There was going to be no quick fix. I would take the time to absorb the profound teachings being offered, years if necessary – learn by them, but above all *change* by them and transform myself into a different spiritual state.

To seek enlightenment seemed rather a pretentious phrase – there is today a lot of pretense and posing in the enlightenment industry. But—as Buddha might have put it—I would not seek the path to flying. In my case flying was to be the path.

"Howdy!" said a voice, suddenly from nowhere.

I looked around and could see no-one.

"It's me pardner, the rowan tree talking to ya!"

Whoa, I thought to myself; I'm going crazy. All this immersion in other dimensions and unnatural fields of consciousness must be having a bad effect. But the voice was loud and clear.

Maybe the intense training and the attempts at transforming my state of mind were making me unstable. That's it! I told myself I was imagining things, because of all the strange mind-bending ideas that had been pumped into me over the last year.

I mean, a talking tree? Ha! Let's talk back and see what happens!

"Why do you have an American accent?"

"I thought it would just liven up your day."

"I can just about cope with the idea of a talking tree, at least in my imagination. But shouldn't you be talking in a Scottish accent, for goodness' sake?"

"I can do a French accent if you like," he said defensively. "*Chacun a son gout, c'est c'est bon…*"

"No please, American is fine. I'm sorry I was rude."

I shook my head and tried to clear my thoughts. But nothing changed. I do believe I was getting telepathic messages from a tree. Best fit with the evidence, anyway. Well, what the hell has that got to do with flying without wings?

"Do you talk to many visitors like this?"

"No, but I could tell straight away you were a tree person."

"I love trees, certainly," I replied cautiously.

"Goody. I've heard about tree huggers; I've been dying to meet one."

"Where did you get that California accent?"

"The big redwoods."

"You talk to them?"

"Of course, all trees talk to one another, no matter the distance. And, of course, to trees past."

"What do you mean, trees past?"

"Ghosts. They are still here. Trees never go away completely. There was a fine old Caledonian forest where Glasgow now stands. I talk to them sometimes. They miss the birds and the wild."

"And where are these trees now?"

"Still in Glasgow, of course. There is a great old pine, thousands of years old, right by the corner of West Nile Street and St Vincent Street. The traffic now is doing him in, poor thing; the noise and the terrible fuel pollution. I suppose you know oil products came from us trees, hundreds of millions of years ago."

This was too much. I didn't feel I could cope with tree ghosts and decided to change the subject. "I suppose you must have seen a lot of the life here, before the glen was cleared?"

"Not me. I was just a berry when the people left but my ancestors told me everything."

"I know the Gaelic tradition that the rowan tree protects the household in its shelter from harm."

"It didn't do much good here, did it?" he sighed.

"But you did your best in a fast-changing world, I'm sure. Don't be so hard on yourself."

"I'll try to be brave about it. But you don't know how lonely it is sometimes, standing here without the chatter and bustle, the laughter of children or the music that was sung. All I hear day in day out is the rumble of the sea and the wind sighing with memories."

"I'm sure it must be very different for you here today than in former times."

"We rowans were always very proud of our custodian of the people tradition."

"The families may all be scattered, gone to the New World. But they are still there, in a very real sense. Can't you talk to other trees and help your clan people indirectly?"

"Networking you mean? Oh yes, I've heard of that too! Well, I could try. Do you think it would work?"

"I'm sure it's worth a try."

This was one very insecure tree. What did that make me, an arbo-psychiatrist or a New Age nut?

"Well, I can't stay all day. It's been nice talking to you."

"Just a minute, before you go..." chipped in another voice.

"What?"

"It's me, the big stone you are sitting on."

This was too much. I sat still, hoping the illusion would go away.

"I'm not leaving," it said, as if reading my mind.

"Look, a talking tree is a crazy concept but at least a tree is alive..."

I'm sure I heard a big, sad sigh at that point.

"OK, so tell me you are alive!"

"You're talking with me," was the chiding reply.

"That could mean I'm hallucinating, not that you are alive."

"You might be hallucinating but I'm here, thinking and talking..."

That was possibly true.

"So how long have you been able to think and talk?"

"Not long."

Then it suddenly hit me, in a giddy rush that made me feel quite weak and very peculiar: I was imbuing trees and stones with consciousness. It was me!

Somehow I had developed so many strange and subtle powers with my journey into flying, that I was able to flow consciousness into the outer reality. I could wake up rocks and stones! As a test, I made the thought of withdrawing my consciousness from the tree and the stone.

There was silence. I waited a full fifteen minutes and there was not a peep from either.

It seemed petty to leave things like that and so I reversed my test conditions.

"Thanks, Doc," said the tree.

"Yes, thank you," piped up the stone.

"How did you know I'm a doctor? I never told you..." Even as I said it, I felt stupid. If it was my consciousness breathing life into the landscape, of course they knew I was a doctor. They probably knew the color of my underwear and my taste in women.

"Blue and blue," they said at the same time.

"What are you talking about?"

"Blue underpants," said the stone.

"And feeling blue about someone you once loved very dearly, who so far hasn't been replaced in your affections."

This was creepy. It was time to go. After this unnerving experience, I did not want to get back to my car after dark. On the wild strath of Suardal, I thought it very likely that the one-legged Ludag would show up and start kicking my ass till I went mad. Today I could believe in goblins, for sure.

"I have to go, you guys. But have a good time when I'm gone."

"We will," said the stone.

"Been nice meeting you both."

"The pleasure was all mine," said the tree. "You'll come again?" he added, diffidently.

"I'm sure. This is such a lovely place and I find great peace and beauty here. Perhaps more so, now that the people are gone."

"Well, goodbye."

"Goodbye."

The stone simply fell silent. But I felt sorry for the tree. He sounded as if the sap was overflowing.

I looked away quickly and strode off in the direction of the western end of the bay and took the shoreline path to my favourite waterfall. It was a very rocky and tough scramble, there being no beach. Half the time it felt like mountaineering, not a walk along the strand.

It took nearly an hour to reach the place I had chosen long ago as a retreat. Here one of the gurgling burns running down the flanks of Beinn Bhuidhe reached the sea abruptly. The energies released as the water tumbled over the eighty foot cliff were awesome to appreciate. On windy days the spray was spun into a misty veil of such beauty that I ached to look on it.

It seemed only right, therefore, that as I descended into a personal grief after the loss of my first wife, that this would be the mystical doorway that took me back to happier times. I chose this spot for my entry into the shamans' Middle World and set aside there a feast of memories and a vision of her as she once was, young and lovely, which I could turn to when the loneliness was too bitter to endure.

For make no mistake, this other world is there, as real as our own, but just beyond reach. I need a certain skill and mind-set to step across into the Middle World but I had practiced it sufficiently.

I found the fond memories again and nourished myself a little from my larder of love. For once I was not suffering. But I couldn't help thinking of the poor tree and his bitter-sweet memories for a past that would never return.

For Boreraig had died.

For the reader:

If you are a tree-hugger: do it again! You know it feels good.

If you are open to it, sit under a tree and listen for any thoughts that might come. You could be surprised.

If all this nonsense appals you, try at least to sense the life energy of a tree. It is measurable scientifically and extends outwards several metres. You don't have to be psychic to feel it. Just stand near the tree until you feel something impinging. You may need to try several trees. Some have stronger auras than others. Obviously this works best in spring and summer, when the trees' energy is at its highest.

If you want to get scientific, read the research of Harold Saxton Burr and rig some trees up to electrometers. You'll soon see the life force (L-field) that he discovered.

19. One night in the emergency room

Back at work, I had little time for thoughts on flying in the next few weeks. My A and E colleague was forced to take extended sick leave and his locum was not sufficiently experienced to be left entirely alone. The moratorium on the path to flying came to an end abruptly one night, with events beyond my control.

I was nearing the end of a long weekend shift; almost fifty hours had passed by and just over twelve hours to go as first on call. Needless to say I was pretty exhausted mentally and physically and looking forward to a good rest after logging off the next day. Meanwhile, I was hoping for a relaxed night shift. There are sometimes nights which are so quiet that, despite being on call, the MO might get a good night's sleep.

But it was not to be. Disaster struck about eight in the evening, just after the nurses had changed shifts. An urgent phone call from the ambulance service informed us that they were attending a highway pile up and there were many injured, some dead, some critical. We had to gear up fast for large numbers.

It happens from time to time, of course. But in the state I was in I could perhaps have wished it was any night but this one. I issued the necessary instructions to my team and then ordered a strong coffee. The patients tonight would need blood, bandages and stitches; the doctor would need several transfusions of caffeine to keep going – a dangerous upper and a bad downer.

"I'm sorry Doc," said the nursing sister with a sympathetic smile.

"It's OK. I just tell myself it could be me they are bringing here in a rubber bag. Self pity soon evaporates!"

In what seemed like no time, a series of claxons could be heard and less than a minute later the first trolley was wheeled in rapidly through the double flap doors. From then on it was non-stop until beyond midnight: quick assessment; stop the bleeding; off to x-ray then back for patching up, bandages and morphine. "Next!"

Seven were critical and we lost three of them but there was no time to react, beyond the feeling of helplessness. It seemed for a time like an endless tide of injuries, blood and fear. Soon, despite the frequent changing of gowns, my underclothes were soaked with blood. I'm sorry to say that on one occasion I forgot to put on fresh gloves when I went from one patient to the next, such was the speed we worked for the first three hours. I was feeling groggy long before midnight, despite the two junior surgical officers drafted in to help.

The team was magnificent throughout-calm, efficient, coordinated and, above all, reassuring. Even Father Roberts, the hospital padre, aware that a crisis had burst upon us, rolled up his sleeves and joined in to help, pushing trolleys, comforting those who needed it, running to and fro with refreshments, and he even lent a hand with the bandaging as best he could.

"Thank you, Father," I said when I had a moment to do so.

"It's nothing, Doctor. I know God has a quota system but I doubt he would want so many at once!" he grinned.

Eventually, as it must, the eye of the storm passed and the pressure we were under noticeably decreased. I later learned we had seen twenty three cases, of which only three were fatally injured and one left on a life support machine. She was still there when I last checked, almost a year later.

"Doctor, would you please tell us what to do with the man in cubicle six?" one of the nursing sisters asked me apologetically around midnight. She could see I was all in.

"What do we know about him?" I said.

"I think he's OK. No fractures, no whiplash, no bleeding and no signs of a head injury. But he looks shocking."

He certainly did when I saw him. He was shaking and looked so pale that he might have had severe internal bleeding. But his vital signs gave no clue that anything was amiss.

"What do you want us to do, put him on a thirty minute special?"

Something told me there was more to be learned before deciding what to do with him.

"How do you feel?" I said to the patient, stalling while I had time to take in his overall condition.

"No trouble. No trouble at all, Doctor," he said with a lilting Irish accent. I would have said he was drunk, or I'm no judge.

"Well, I was going to let you go home but you look pretty shocked. Maybe we'll keep you under observation for a few more hours."

"It's not the accident, Doctor. I was sitting in the back seat and barely grazed meself. But they brought me in here anyway. I felt fine. But when the priest came and I saw his dog collar, I thought 'Feck me!' I'm dying sure enough. He's here to give me the last rites. That's enough to shock a body twice out of his wits."

He shook his head sorrowfully, showing great perplexity.

"Well then, you can leave," I said, trying to keep a straight face." The padre was helping me tonight, not the Holy One up there!" I pointed past the ceiling. The poor man seemed much more himself.

As we watched him go, praising the Virgin Mary that he was saved after all, the nurse and I finally burst into peals of laughter. Everyone wanted to know what was so funny, amidst such mayhem. When they were told, they too erupted with giggles. It was one of the lighter events that helped the final hours pass swiftly.

There it might have ended, a hectic night dealing with casualties mangled in a multiple road traffic accident. I retired wearily to my room, in expectation of a just and proper sleep.

But an hour later I was woken by an urgent call from A and E. I dressed quickly; the brisk walk of a few minutes in the night air woke me sufficiently to perform adequately. There was another broken and bleeding figure lying on the trolley, with nurses putting up a dextrose line, pending my decision.

"What happened here?" I asked the paramedic, who had arrived in conjunction with the patient.

"We picked him up after a bad fall from a second floor balcony. Apparently he had gone whacko on LSD and decided he could fly! He launched himself over the railings to prove his point." There was a heavy sarcasm in his voice.

"Any relations or friends here?"

"Everyone at the party was stoned, only one in a fit state to call an ambulance. Those who were off with the fairies were sectioned and taken to the psychiatric ward. The rest were rounded up by the police and taken into custody…" He looked at me and hesitated. "Are you allright Doctor?"

This paramedic could not possibly have known why the language of his report was so shocking to me.

"Yes," I muttered in a daze. "I'm fine."

I realized this was no time to move into emotional over-stimulation and snapped myself out of it with a deep breath, before going to attend to the victim.

In fact he was remarkably unhurt from his fall. But as he regained consciousness more and more, it became clear he was still in a psychotic state, and would attempt to fly again, if unattended.

Strictly speaking, the correct action for a physician at this point was to sign a custody order under section four of the 1983 Mental Health Act; that is forcibly admit him short-term to a psychiatric ward for his own protection, as a point of law. You can imagine my dilemma. Why was this man sick yet I wasn't? OK, he took LSD. As a result he imagined he could overturn the laws of physics and fly without wings.

It was the moment of decision.

Later that night, I awoke from a restless sleep to hear a voice.

"Is there a problem, Doctor?"

As I struggled to wakefulness, with the burden of very long hours still weighing me down, I suddenly realized: it was the fairy!

But there was no form.

"Where are you? Show yourself."

"We thought you would not need a physical manifestation."

"I suppose not."

"We sensed there was worry, confusion."

"Doubts, yes, certainly."

"You will readily accept that we create our own doubts and confusions?"

"Yes."

"Do we not then create situations in which those doubts are manifest?"

"Are you suggesting I created the patient who wanted to fly but was manifestly insane?"

"I am."

"That's crazy! I can accept the idea of Fate or what Jung called synchronicity. But not that I am able yet to create reality to that degree."

"Is the event itself not proof enough of the powers of your consciousness, whether recognized or not?"

To this there was no convincing answer. The Cosmos seemed to be challenging me. Or perhaps just trying to teach me something I was reluctant to learn. Maybe that was why I was so shocked when presented with the events of the night: at some level, deep down, I knew that I was gaining powers and wanted to put the brakes on.

"It's not just a question of whether it is proper, sane or moral to fly. I'm not even sure I will ever have the ability to fly."

"Try to recover your determination, Doctor, of which I have no doubts. You have been an earnest soul this night, suffering for the good of others. Sleep will calm you of fears and in the morning things may look very different."

"I suppose you will just tell me success is a matter of persistence?"

"Doctor, persistence will give you almost anything–eventually." He pronounced the last word with evident distaste. "They say that if you set a thousand monkeys to work, each with a typewriter, then sooner or later, one of them will type the complete works of Shakespeare. That's perseverance at work. But it isn't a sensible way to write a book."

"OK, point taken. Think smart, not think hard, as people say."

"Not where I come from," he sniffed. "But you seem to have grasped the gist of what I am saying."

"Really you're saying that flying is a creative act. If I sit on a mountain forever, I'll never fly. Even if an earthquake eventually tipples me off, that isn't flying!"

I have no idea if or what he replied: I was already fast asleep!

For the reader:

Reflect on the times that you wanted something and didn't get it. Write them down. Now against each, list all your creations which blocked you from getting what you wanted. This is negative thinking but at least acknowledge yourself for your powers of manifestation!

From this day, start trying to magnetize things towards yourself that you wish and *do not block the thought.* You will be surprised at what comes; just be determined.

Then pay special attention to the lesson of the next chapter!

20. The Three Wishes Phenomenon

I dreamed a lot about mysterious places. Nothing was as it had been. For one moment I was out in space, in the deepest blackest part, and came upon a hole of terrifying size and madness. It burned with a black heat and as I was drawn into it, it seared me with such a dreadful burning ache, I scarcely wanted to be conscious ever again, for fear of encountering that pain in other ways.

I woke sweating but supposing I was free of the nightmare.

This was not the case. Night after night I dreamt it and many other awesome realities that were not meant for Man.

I was treading in dangerous places and being made to feel unwelcome. Even my own thoughtscape had become alien. After days without sleep I finally collapsed and took a rest. This was my own spiritual emergency!

I was granted a few days of sick leave. I hurried north to Skye yet again. It was a flaming September, ablaze with the autumn colours of red, orange, gold and yellow. The bracken on the hills had gone from green to gold and the heather was at its peak of purple hue. The waters of every loch and sea inlet were filled with crystallized and marbled blue, shimmering lazily in the dazzle of autumn sunlight. Likewise the distant islands were blue, sea and land merging into a watercolour monochrome. It was more Mediterranean than that mother of all seas – were it not for the sharp cold air.

I knew where I would find him, or rather I suppose he told me in some way, across the distance. In no time I was sitting by him, pouring out my doubts and fears.

"Perhaps I'm not meant to fly," I said to him, heavy with sadness.

Notice how we weigh ourselves down with black thoughts—depression surely describes a physical condition—being pressed or pushed down. By contrast we speak of being "light as a feather" and "free as a bird" when we rejoice and are released from our troubles and cares. Until this moment, I never associated such emotional changes with the sense of weight. Of course this would interfere with flying.

"It's really very simple. You are continuing to make it complicated."

"But humans are not meant to fly. Do you know any others who can?"

"No, I do not."

"Well, there you are then."

"You are being foolish. I've only met two other human beings in over a century. Neither of them professed an interest in learning to fly."

"Maybe it's me. I'm just useless."

He stood up quickly and looked very stern.

"If you ever speak in those terms before me again, I shall leave and never return."

"What terms?" I was alarmed by his sudden change in mood and countenance.

"Using verbal language to destroy yourself and your creation. In nothing are humans more foolish and irritating than this. The difference between a wise person and an average human being is that a wise person will continue to support his or her viewpoint, no matter the vicissitudes. Their view of themselves and their Being is as sacred as respect for the divine Higher Spirit. Humans so often resort to petulant rages in which they attack their own powers and creations, like mad animals tearing up the furniture of their own home."

"I'm sorry."

"To be sorry is not enough. I have spent months trying to teach you to believe in your own powers and in seconds you undo anything I might have achieved. Now do you see why people from the Other World so rarely have time and patience to deal with humans? You say one thing and mean another. That makes it difficult for any friend or teacher, no matter how much love and compassion we feel."

"We're pretty unrewarding, huh?"

He nodded.

"But I do want to fly, I really do. It means so much to me."

"Then why wish it away in a few careless words? You wish trouble and failure upon yourself."

"The words just came out; I didn't mean what I said. It certainly wasn't a wish."

"But it was," he said in an exasperated tone of voice. "Humans have a great deal of trouble with this subject of wishes or intentions. Let me explain a powerful truth to you. *There is no problem getting your wishes to come true.* The awful truth is that you ALWAYS get what you ask for. The Cosmos is kind like that. It's just that people insist on asking for the wrong things."

"But if I say I'm lousy at French grammar, that isn't a wish!"

"Of course it is, man! It is a verbal construction which changes the future. How else would you define a wish?" he said gravely.

"It doesn't mean I truly desire to have a future that way."

"No, but the danger you don't see is that you have to create that concept in your own mind, before giving voice to it. Now, I have been telling you almost since the day we met that the power of your mind is capable of giving to you anything it creates. To abuse that power giving thought to self-destructive creations, even unintentionally, is a kind of mental vandalism."

"Well, how do I stop it?"

"The first requirement is simply to become aware of your 'inner' voice and listen to yourself speaking. You can have someone else note down what you are saying for a day. You will notice that many times you make counter-intelligent utterances, negative statements and disempowering phrases and wishes: "I wish I was dead," or have you ever said, "I have a terrible memory", "I'm broke," or "Nobody seems to care"? You are wishing things upon yourselves constantly, through conversation and internal dialogue. You may think you are just describing your life as it is. **But you are actually creating your life through these wishes or beliefs."**

"But most people have trouble making their wishes stick. Why is this such a contradiction?"

"The key is clarity. Most people have trouble getting what they want because they are not thinking clearly and unequivocally what it is they are seeking. They make wishes and then confuse the Cosmos by counteracting them with subsequent newer or second wishes."

"I'm not following you."

"A person, say, wishes he was rich."

"What's the problem with that?"

"He has already got his wish but created a second wish "I'm poor", to mask and unmock the first wish. So now he is making a third wish, to be wealthy, not realizing he already has such a wish in place."

"I get it!" I suddenly blurted out. "It's the three wishes!"

"What are you saying?"

"Well, we have kind of tradition; there are many stories, along the same lines, about a man who meets a fairy, a genie, a witch or whatever, and is granted three wishes. And usually, in the story, his first wish is a mistake, such as "I wish everything was made of gold," and so it is. He just blurts out the first thing he thinks of."

"Just like in real life."

"Well, yes. Then he has to use the second wish to undo it all and the third wish is just spent getting back to safety. Or he wastes the last wish saying something typically human and really stupid like, "I wish I knew what it was I wanted most, but I don't". By then all three wishes are used up and it's too late: he now knows what he wants but gets nothing! In good stories the man is now wiser and focuses more clearly on what are the real issues that matter in life."

"Maybe all these fairy tales, as you call them," he sniffed slightly I swear, "Have been trying to tell you something."

"I never understood it until now. The three wishes are just a metaphor for something people do to themselves all the time. I wonder who first thought up these tales? He was very wise."

"Indeed he was."

"So, like the person in the fairy tale, we make the first wish unconsciously, not realizing we already have the power to make wishes come true, that's what you are telling me. Then we make second wishes that countermand these."

"Exactly..."

"Then make a third wish, to get what we think we want, but already had?"

"Just so."

"So my desire to fly is really the third wish, not the first?"

"As I already explained, you had this ability long ago. Then you made a wish, or as you might put it 'changed your belief', and decided you could no longer fly."

"So people who make affirmations are really trying to outsmart their own mistaken wishes?"

"Usually, yes."

"It would be better to stop making lousy wishes in the first place?"

"Exactly. All such negative, destructive and limiting statements are wrong by definition, since they conflict with the natural order of things, which is joy, goodness and abundance."

My head began to spin with the importance of this latest revelation. The implications for therapy are staggering. To find and strip off the second unwanted wish will help many patients solve their anxiety and neurosis.

"What I have just told you applies widely to all illness."

"You mean, not just psychiatric problems?"

"All sick people who are suffering, wish to regain their health. That's the third wish. But the illness was the second, negative wish, made in some moment of despair or distress, so undoing their first wish…"

"Which is a long and happy life!"

"Just so."

I gasped as the truth of this struck home.

That night in my lodgings, I brainstormed all the negative second wishes about flying I could think of. There were plenty…

Note:

Weeks later I tried this with a patient who had cancer. She realized her tumour was a second wish against her husband. She had kept saying to him "You make me sick", then obligingly gone ahead and made that "wish" come true. Within days of this realization the patient had come back from the precipice of death and within weeks the tumour had regressed sufficiently to astonish the oncologist.

She eventually fully recovered.

Suggestion for reader:

Tape record your own conversations and listen for damning negative wishes. You'll be shocked and amazed. Stop doing it to yourself. You'll be even more amazed at the improvements in your life.

Recall times in your life you have wished for something desirable. Write these down. Then try to go behind these wishes and identify the second wish that destroyed the first "wish" you already had! Remember, the third wish is the "solution", the second wish is the deadly killer.

For example, if you wish to lose weight (third wish), the second wish might be: "Yum! Yum! I love food!"

Knocking out the second wish is key, not strengthening the third wish! As soon as you spot the second wish that ruined what you had, erase it from your psyche. Note: You don't need to do anything to the first wish. Just kiss it better and love it back to life!

Don't be surprised if you get a miracle (and if you do, write and tell me about it).

Go through your affirmations list and delete all those which are obviously third wishes (which is all of them). Then dig out the second wish and erase it for each. You'll be back in the natural uncorrupted state—infinite abundance, joy and wisdom.

21. Learning To Leave The Body Behind

As if fate intended it, when I returned south from Skye, I came across an interesting technique for changing states of consciousness from a magazine article written by Australian writer Jacqueline Parkhurst of "*Open Mind Publications*". It was said to enable people to leave their bodies, and travel into other dimensions.

Given my interest in shamanism, it was natural that I would experiment with the method. Three people are required, one subject and two helpers. It was easy to persuade my good friend Sister Lynnette, a first class nursing officer, and radiologist Peter to join in.

The subject lies down comfortably on a mattress or cushions on the floor, with bare or stockinged feet. One of the helpers begins to gently massage the feet of the subject, the other helper rubs the subject's forehead vigorously with the edge of the hand.

It is very relaxing at first and soothes down normal external stimuli, creating a deeply introverted state. But after a short while the forehead massage begins to become very insistent. A few more minutes and it creates a buzzing sensation within the head and the subject begins to feel confused and disoriented, after a temporary breakdown of perception and cognitive function.

It is probably the disruption of the normal processes of sensing and thinking that opens the door to altered consciousness and its unusual perceptions. I could not help but remember the words of my mentor: that the spiritual experience only comes in when the mind and brain is shut down. Our endless drive for rational perfection is what mainly stands in the road of our spiritual powers.

When my turn came, I found the induction was very bizarre and unlike anything else I had ever experienced, even with my shamanic travels. In just a few minutes I was ready to put the technique to the test.

Lynette, my guide, reading from the instructions we were provided with, gave me a series of directions to follow:

"Imagine your body growing two inches longer at the feet."

This wasn't difficult and took less than half a minute.

"Now imagine you're two inches longer at the head end."

I signalled that I had done this too.

"Now imagine you are six inches longer at the feet."

I was getting the idea.

"Now imagine you are six inches longer at the head end."

It took a few moments longer but wasn't too difficult, given the strange state of mind I was in. Then I was told to imagine being progressively longer and longer, until I could really feel myself two feet longer at the lower end and then two feet longer at the head end.

"Now picture yourself two feet longer at the feet and two feet longer at the head *simultaneously*," said Lynette.

It took some doing but I found that, with effort, I could induce the sensation of being four feet longer in all.

"Now imagine your body growing in all directions at once, outwards, like a balloon!"

This was much harder and took several minutes. It happened quite suddenly and felt most peculiar. By this time my body and mind were completely out of sync and I had ceased receiving cogent sensory messages via the nervous system. I had just a brief moment to dwell on this and realize that it meant consciousness and the brain had been truly separated.

"Your mind is now separating from the body," Lynette intoned gently. "Now travel through this other space to your own front door." After a suitable pause, she said, "Describe what you see."

This was weird but I found it surprisingly easy. I knew my own front door, of course. Just from memory. But somehow I *knew* that I was seeing it for real, as it was at that moment, not when I last saw it.

"Now raise yourself up to one thousand feet above the ground. Tell me when you are there."

When I was ready I nodded.

"Now turn slowly, through a full circle, describing what you see as you turn."

This I did, describing a familiar environment in considerable detail, yet from an entirely new perspective, which I had never seen before. It suddenly dawned on me that, of course, I really *was* sitting high in the firmament above my own house, not just imagining it. How else could I describe a scene which I had never seen from that angle?

"Now have it alternate light and darkness. Change the scene you see, until you know for sure that it is you creating the experiences."

This sounded like the creative awareness that the fairy had first described all those months ago. Of course, I knew it was me; I was generating the scenery and making it real. Here I was, floating high above the ground, without my body. I was flying, in a sense! If I needed any proof that I was not a body, fully conscious without one and able to create any reality I chose, this was it.

I was in a highly paradoxical state we call dual consciousness, literally in two places at once: aware of my Self and surroundings in the room with my friends but at the same time fully aware as a disembodied spirit, floating free many miles away. This was very different from altered consciousness; I was fully integrated with this reality but in a different point of view. Sceptics would try to argue that this was all just imagination. But the psychologist who had introduced me to this technique had reported a highly interesting event which put paid to any idea that this was just illusion.

The subject was a woman called Julie. Several of her friends were present in the room, apart from the psychologist. Julie was asked to locate an acquaintance, Vivienne, and describe what she was doing in another part of the building. After a pause, Julie stated that she was outside Vivienne's window, looking in. She could see Vivienne, who was talking to a woman she had never seen before. Asked to describe her, Julie said this female visitor had light reddish hair down to her shoulders, a roundish freckled face, and she was about 5'4" tall.

In order to check this story out, the psychologist had whispered to one of the onlookers, a youth called Alistair, to go up and see if anybody was in Vivienne's room. After a couple of minutes, Julie started giving a full physical description of somebody else entering the room, then exclaimed with surprise, "Oh, it's Alistair!" She had been apparently unaware that Alastair had left the room.

A few minutes later Alistair came back with an astounded Vivienne and a girl exactly fitting Julie's description. Vivienne made the psychologist promise never to send anyone spying on her again. This was gold standard paranormal stuff!

Lynnette continued with my transition. "Now, forget all preconceived notions of what might be below, and allow yourself to gently descend to the ground and tell me what reality you encounter. It could be a place, it could be a past life, it could be another dimension, anything."

Down and down I went and touched the ground with the slightest bump. I was in a cave. It seemed somehow familiar.

"Greetings, Doctor. I've been expecting you!"

It was the fairy. I couldn't believe my senses; at least not right away.

"I see you are making significant progress, Doctor. This is good. Very good."

But before I had chance to reply, I found myself being sucked back into ordinary space. I felt heavier and my whole psyche seemed to pour back into my physical form, like a liquid life essence.

Suddenly it was all over and I felt entirely normal again.

Or not quite.

I found I knew something I did not perceive clearly before. I have no idea how this came about. It was, in a sense, a transformation. For me, from that moment, all science lost validity; it is based on a fatal flaw, which is so obvious I wonder it isn't debated in schools (the paradox is well within the rational capabilities of kids).

The paradox is this: *Science assumes that the unknown, which is being sought, will be just like the known we already have.* Now this ridiculous notion may not break down on a very local scale, such as Man and the surrounding pond-life of planet Earth. But on the grand Cosmic scale, such an assumption is unwarranted and frankly outrageous. The Universe is such a vast place we have no right whatever to postulate that it will be identical or even similar in form or workings throughout its whole as it is in the tiny locality we inhabit!

This realization made nonsense of all scientific reasoning because of the critical philosophical flaw which is easy to spot when stated as follows: *the assumption that the unknown is like the known assumes a prior knowledge of the unknown!*

What a hubris!

For the reader:

If you want to try the Christos method, start with G. M. Glaskin's book, entitled "Windows of the Mind: the Christos Experience", Arrow, 1976.

You can also use the technique described here, which is exactly as Glaskin gives it.

22. The Blessed Loch

In November I drove north again. I had decided on this visit to locate an historic place of healing, called *Loch Sianta* or the Holy Well, in north-east Skye. As a doctor I was naturally interested in the remarkable properties of the water of this once-famous well.

According to eighteenth-century historian Martin Martin, *Loch Sianta* was famed far and wide as a specific for many conditions, from headache to consumption and hopeful invalids would travel long distances, which in those days was difficult and sometimes hazardous, in the hope of a magical cure.

Nowadays the site is seldom visited and knowledge of its existence is fast disappearing, along with much other folk lore in Skye. Its name is no longer marked on modern maps and the current Ordnance Survey sheet has even drawn its whereabouts incorrectly, creating confusion and hastening its disappearance from all save the longest memory.

Only by house to house enquiries in the vicinity was I able to locate it. The approach was muddy and unpleasant to walk, where the ground had been churned by grazing animals from the croft nearby. Of human footprints there were none to be seen.

The loch is found in a small amphitheatre only a quarter of a mile from the seashore, drained at its northern end by a swift bubbling stream which tumbles down to the sea. Roughly ten by thirty yards in extent, it is bounded on the west by a steep slope covered in birch, hazel and alder trees, the remainder by a mossy green sward, where occasional rosehip shrubs dipped down to the water's edge. There were supposed to be twenty four springs feeding it, though I could only identify nine. It was practise, I had read in Martin, for visitors to walk three times round the loch in a clockwise direction. It was no longer possible to enact this ritual without becoming fast in the coppice of brambles and tearing clothes or skin.

On the day I visited, the hushed early November sunshine fell aslant the limpid waters, which were crystal clear all the way down, a remarkable thing in itself, when all other lochs in the locality are dark with peat, almost inky. Taking its light from the surroundings, the surface of the pool reflected a shimmering mixture of emerald, malachite, indigo and lime, punctuated with gold and a little crimson, from the fading leaves on the opposite bank.

Across the silvery ethereal sea to the east rose the snow-covered peaks around Loch Broom, Gairloch and Glen Torridon on the Scottish mainland. They were stern and beautiful in the glittering sun shafts that darted among the clouds hanging there like pillows of light. Northwards, the Summer Isles were dark against the snowy background, hidden from the warming rays of the sun. I do not doubt that if Scotland's climate were fairer it would be here, in this land of shimmering illumination and not Tuscany, that the Renaissance artist would have found his inspiration in the refulgent light.

It was clear, from the moment I set foot in the secluded hollow, that I was in a very blessed place. The atmosphere was sizzling with spiritual energies which only the most insensitive individual could fail to detect. Bending down to the stream I washed my face in the holy waters and felt at once their healing energetic properties. It was not a sensation I would ever expect to feel when dispensing a modern chemical medicine!

I walked around and viewed the scene from several angles. I took photographs from which I hoped to make a serene picture for my study wall, to remind me of this visit. One or two fungi were so colourful and ornamental that I squatted low to photograph these too. I had almost finished and was quite disappointed that he had failed to show, for few places on the island could have a more supernatural connection than this, when a sudden shadow told me he was there.

"Good morning, Doctor!"

As I turned to face him and return his greeting, I noticed that the backlight revealed a considerable aura extending outwards several feet from his human form. I was tempted for a brief moment to try to take a surreptitious photograph.

"Don't do it, Doctor."

"I only hesitated when the thought appeared. I wouldn't have taken it without your permission."

"What would it prove? You are still clinging to the common reality, though I have repeatedly stated that this is your trap."

"I'm sorry," I said contritely. "You must be very impatient with my slow learning."

"Impatience is a time-based word. I have an infinity of time. You are the one with the mortality problem, Doctor."

I was not comfortable with sarcasm from a higher power and as for the humour, it was about as bleak as a John Knox sermon. I showed my dissatisfaction with a scowl.

"Come, let us walk," he said, ignoring my petulance.

We set off towards the shore, past the stone where small offerings were once left by visiting hopefuls. The ground was very wet and boggy and I had to detour at several places, to avoid sinking up to my ankles in mud. He seemed to simply glide over the ground with little more than a dent in the grasses.

"Look," I said, changing the mood. "There are signs of fairy activity around here."

"What makes you say that?"

"Toadstools, lots of them. It always means fairies are near. I'm sure if we keep quiet we may see one!"

"Very droll, Doctor."

We came to sit, at last, on rocky seats on the shore. There were many fossils of belemnites to be seen in the soft shale near the outlet of the healing waters.

"Once upon a time I would have thought of these as very old," I commented, fingering the relic of millions of years ago. "Now it seems like time is stretched out on such a vast scale that it means very little to me now."

"When you attain pure consciousness, Doctor, it will mean nothing at all."

"I hear this term pure consciousness a lot. It's a bit of a cliché. The people who talk about it definitely don't have it, that's for sure."

"You are astute Doctor. Those who write and talk about it have no inkling of what they claim to know. Meaningless pap."

"But what about masters, spiritual adepts? There are such people, of course – I mean not just folk like yourself, disguised as humans!"

"But they are the least likely to talk of it. They may demonstrate their capability but would hardly boast."

"But you have chosen to reveal truths to me."

"No, Doctor, you chose me. Are you aware of the saying that when a man is ready to travel to the ends of the earth to find truth, his teacher will appear close by?"

I must have looked down bashfully.

"Doctor, do you think I would have wasted my time by selecting a human at random and hoping to educate him concerning his true nature?"

"Put that way, it does sound stupid, yes."

At that moment a crackling light came within and I was startled. I could only attribute it to the energies of his presence acting upon my neurological system. It occurred to me that this was a lot to do with guru worship in those parts of the world where the teacher is beloved for his very self, as well as his knowledge. Perhaps some transformation could be passed one to another by direct transfer, like some miraculous light that is switched on in another soul.

I framed this as a question to my mentor.

"There is a connection, a link formed yes. More a oneness emerging than a transference, as you put it. The presence of another being can be helpful in many ways."

"I mean, if a being has become hypnotized into the game of life in the physical world, it is going to take a second presence to help undo the implanted message of being trapped and without choice, isn't it?"

"Agreed. But remember the presence of a guru or teacher, therapist or whatever you want to call it may be invisible. There are many connections in your life, with many influences. Some you may not be aware of but are working for your benefit. Some may be as little as a few spoken words within your hearing. Sometimes the message is only for the attuned listener, even though everyone present hears the words, no-one else understands their true meaning."

"Radio Cosmos! I'm just the wireless receiver."

"Something like that," he smiled and caught my gaze. He reached for my hands and held them gently for a few moments. This was only the second time we had touched.

I felt tears begin to prick at my eyes. Oh God, how embarrassing!

For the reader:

Try this experiment, to see if the idea of a living universe means anything to you: Just quietly out of doors, quite alone where you will not be disturbed, locate a rock or large stone and sit down by it. Try to put yourself into the body and being of the stone. Be the stone, feel like a stone (here's where the incredible power of the human mind comes in useful).

Listen for words or ideas coming back at you from the stone. Say "Hello," be friendly. You'll be surprised how often this pays off.

Once in a while you may meet a sad or tired being who knew better days but is now turning solid, away from its non-material nature. Talk to it and raise its enthusiasm for life. Suggest that it could move up a little, into some kind of sentient creature, and try to nudge it to depart and do so.

Don't give up too soon if it doesn't come easily. Try different stones, different localities and different days or seasons!

23. The New Fourth Dimension

A few days later, I traveled to the mystical site of Callanish, on the Outer Hebridean isle of Lewis. This is a stone circle, in the Stonehenge tradition, which stands on a rise and, unlike its more famous southern counterpart, is visible from a wide area around. The word *nish* or *neis* is from the Viking language (Norse) and means rock or stone.

I first saw it decades ago, lonely and wild, but today visitor numbers are such that a path has been laid around the perimeter of the site by Historic Scotland, to lessen the damage of constant footprints to the monument.

Callanish is now the focus of visits at the summer solstice, from what might be termed earth mystery tourists or perhaps neo-pagans! They are hoping to connect with the Cosmic energies of fire which surface here and may give rise to the energetic being known as the "Shining One", which is said to walk among the stones at certain times.

Now this legend could be a folk memory recalling the astronomical significance of the stones; perhaps it was not a person but a planet or supernova? See, there I go again with my lateral thinking…

Great power and glory is given to the Druidical tradition, in despite of the Church's opposition. But old beliefs die hard, here in the far west of Europe. After all, do we not stand on the shore, almost within sight of the magical land of *Tir nan Og*, the land of the forever-young?

I had no particular idea in mind for my visit but felt, somehow, that a "connection" was in order.

Nobody knows who placed the stones here but they date from three to four thousand years ago, which is clearly pre-Druids. Local legend trumps science, however, for is it not true that a number of giants who lived on the island refused to be converted to Christianity by Saint Kieran and were therefore promptly turned into stone as a punishment?

For centuries the stones, of Lewisian gneiss (named for this island), were buried in peat up to about the height of an adult. Then in 1857 they were stripped and laid bare, in all their present glory. The central stones particularly are woven like a stone fabric, with threads and seams clearly visible. Maybe this is what the giants were wearing the day they were turned to stone!

Whoever erected them, I can declare they are alive with energies, unlike Stonehenge, which I found dead and cold, despite the reverence lavished upon the more famous monolith by those who believe in Earth mysteries.

In fact I became so acutely aware of an other-worldly presence that reality began to shift. It was a strange feeling, like standing in the middle of an earthquake and feeling the ground turn to jelly. I looked around to see if any other visitors were feeling it. There were just a handful of people but they seemed quite unconcerned.

For them at least, there was nothing out of the ordinary this day.

But I was not like other people any more. The fairy had dragged me so far out of my consciousness sphere, that I was almost off the map and language, never mind place names, had run out long ago.

Suddenly, I was aware of an intense light, coming from the south. Again, nobody else seemed to see anything and they continued their tour and musings uninterrupted. But I was aware of some powerful energy, clothed in light, like a robe. It grew and grew before me, as I gazed in awe and fear. Perhaps it was the "Shining One", come to check me out?

But no, that was a conceited and unworthy thought. In fact I gradually formed the idea this was something from deep space, perhaps connected with the astronomical leanings of the site, after all. Was it a comet, a planet, a star? I couldn't tell. But it seemed to be tugging at me, trying to draw me away from Earth.

I shuddered and was a little afraid. I decided to leave but I saved my dignity by telling myself it was getting dark and I had to get back to the ferry that night, or forfeit my car berth and be marooned on the island for the whole weekend.

At around two in the morning, I woke with a terrible sense of dread, pouring sweat. I had seen a new fourth dimension! Not time – but an undiscovered physical direction. I had read Peter Ouspenky's views, years before on what he called the "fourth dimension." This was before Einstein's imposition of time as the necessary fourth dimension to his new relative universe. In Ouspensky's words "*The conquest of the air; hearing and seeing at a distance; establishing connections with other planets or with other solar systems; all this is nothing in comparison with the discovery of a new dimension.*"

Yet I believed that night I had seen one.

My problem with time as the supposed fourth dimension is that, although it is considered to extend to infinity in both directions, one cannot *travel* it in both directions; only forward along the arrow. This violates a basic property of all other dimensions. The simplest dimension is a line; one can move in either direction along this line to infinity. The plane surface, two dimensions, can expand in any and all directions outwards in that plane and return in the same directions. Three-dimensional space, at least as we experience it, goes out infinitely in all directions. I therefore reject time as an actual dimension; it remains merely a qualitative element of our interaction with space, objects and energy.

What I found myself visualizing is infinite in both directions and fits neatly in a sequence, after the first three. It also had the important property described by Ouspensky that it lies perpendicular to the existing three dimensions, at least in a manner of speaking I will explain. Therefore I believe this is the true fourth dimension. Those who want to hang onto time in this context must in any case reclassify it as number five.

My new dimension is one of scale – smaller and smaller to larger and larger. Let me state at the outset this does not mean smaller and smaller distances within the present three dimensions. It means *growing* smaller and smaller or expanding infinitely. It is at once obvious and in full view, yet missed entirely because we can only see a small aspect of this key dimension.

It becomes confused with the existing three dimensions.

True, people have hinted at it, remarking as William Blake did in the eighteenth century, of smaller and smaller universes within the existing one; "*to hold infinity in the palm of your hand, and eternity in an hour.*" He likened the world to a grain of sand. The fact remains that no-one has ever spotted this as a key new dimension.

I could not wait to meet again with my mentor friend and begin discussions on this new breakthrough. We met at the little ruined church at Trumpan, in northern Skye. It was here one Sunday in May 1578 that the MacDonalds of Uist surrounded the church, while the MacLeods of the nearby village were at worship, and set fire to it. It was an inexcusable act which Scottish author Derek Cooper described as "one of the most sordid atrocities in a time distinguished for its sordid atrocities" (the Scots have traditionally treated each other far worse than they claim the English did!) All save one of the congregation perished in the flames. One woman escaped, although mortally wounded, and raised the alarm.

MacLeod and his army hastened to the scene in wrath and caught the MacDonald's on the shore, where fate had spited them by marooning their galleys on the receding tide. The Fairy Flag of the clan was unfurled and in the vengeful fury which ensued the MacDonalds were slaughtered to a man. Their reviled bodies were heaped into a dyke and covered in stones. That day was ever after known as the Battle of the Spoiled Dyke and MacCrimmon composed a vaunting commemorative tune for the bagpipes.

Over the centuries a deep and lasting peace has come to rest in this lugubrious place that belies its history of evil and blood. The MacLeods and their neighbours continue to be buried here beside the roofless ruins, in a tranquil graveyard which looks out onto the blue Minch and the distant islands of the Outer Hebrides. Here one may sometimes catch sight of a fairy or sprite, as their invisible cloak is momentarily tugged aside by the ceaseless grieving wind.

I explained the vision to him; he understood at once what I was driving at. He set me difficult questions, which forced me to clarify what I was trying to describe.

"Why is this different from merely reducing in size within the existing framework?"

"To merely grow smaller and smaller would be to disappear, eventually. What I am talking about, let's call it the "shrinking dimension", would not change proportion at all. Although you might be in surroundings smaller than the smallest subatomic particle, the proportion or ratio from the tip of your nose to the end of your finger would be just as large."

"And the same in the opposite direction?"

"Of course. That's what convinces me it is a true new dimension. You can go smaller and smaller and smaller, to infinity. Larger and larger and larger, to infinity." Once again the unnerving feeling came to me. I tried to blank out the perception of what it might be like to grow smaller and smaller *to infinity; diminishing for ever and ever.* Somehow this was much more frightening than growing larger and larger.

"Why do you suppose that is, Doctor?" the fairy asked, picking up on my anxiety.

"I'm not sure. Perhaps because when growing bigger and bigger, one does not think of disappearing. But smaller and smaller raises the idea of vanishing into nothing."

"But that cannot happen with your new dimension, Doctor."

"Exactly. It's both confirmatory and alarming. It would be impossible to disappear!"

"Well, I'm impressed, Doctor, because consciousness too cannot disappear. It cannot choose oblivion. There is no possible "death". Hence re-incarnation. Is this not also a scary thought, Doctor? If not, why not?"

"It doesn't raise the same fears. Because the ultimate fear, I suppose, is to unexist. That would be the true end of a being. We already talked about how modern Man has himself believing that he does not exist. But deep down he knows the nature of consciousness, as you have taught me."

"What about perpendicularity?" he challenged me. "How can you describe this as perpendicular to the existing three dimensions, as any new dimension must be?"

"It requires stepping off the existing three in an entirely new direction. I visualize in-and-out as a ninety degree angle *into a different dimension.* Can't you see?" I asked excitedly.

"Doctor, I can vizualize many more dimensions that you can understand. It is from these other dimensions of reality that what you call magic and the false supposition of time are obtained. I am only concerned with your line of argument as it will be understood by your fellow men and women."

"Most people will reject this at first because they can only conceive of retaining the same scale or perspective themselves and seeing objects get smaller and smaller. But to reduce on the existing three dimensions would be merely to arrive at a point; a zero, mathematically, with no dimensions at all."

"And you argue that on your new addition to the matrix nothing would disappear?"

"That's the key. Take the cube defined by three dimensions; if this gets smaller and smaller it is not the same cube moving through a dimension but a series of different cubes, infinitely scaled, following on one after the other. In my new dimension, there would only be one cube and it would change infinitely but remain always exactly the same size at our intersection of this matrix. As it disappears in size it has merely gone off in a different dimension!"

"Do you then argue that we would be unable to see objects that have drifted from us in this new dimension?"

"I would formerly have said impossible. Like the beings of Flatland could not see anything above their world, because it was in the invisible third dimension, I would have argued that we are essentially three-dimensional beings and could not see into this fourth."

"But now you perceive differently?"

"I do. Let me reason it this way: we may be able to travel measurable distances in the existing three dimensions but would soon lose sight of objects further away in any particular direction. Objects infinitely far away could be reached in theory but not visible from here, so to speak. That's a question of light gathering. For the same reason, in this new dimension we may only be able to see a small section of the dimension, objects suitably large or small would simply be beyond our gaze. But definitely there, should we make the effort to travel."

"The important point is that you can conceive of them."

"Exactly. So I believe that my consciousness, at least, has fourth dimensional capabilities."

"Excluding time?"

"Without considering time."

"I like this, Doctor. Your consciousness is growing in strange ways but it is as we would wish."

Back home, I decided to talk this through with my friend Charles and get a physics or mathematics perspective.

Charles listened carefully and sympathetically over a beer. I could see he was having a struggle grasping how this was different to just smaller and smaller. Finally, I think he got it.

"You're not talking Charles Howard Hinton's cubes or Reimann's geometry?" he asked.

"I know what those are. No."

"So shrinking forever, beyond the Planck length?" he asked.

"What is the Planck length?" I asked him.

"The Planck length is supposed to be the smallest real measurement obtainable in our present universe. Beyond that reality has no meaning."

"Why?" I challenged him. I'd decided to be difficult!

"The best way of thinking about that is to imagine everything to start touching."

"Well, isn't there a version of Zeno's paradox kicks in here?" I asked him. "Every time you halve the distance between two particles, you can halve it again, then again, then again and again and again. It never ends. You can always halve the remaining distance so the two particles never touch?"

"Well, in your own words, Zeno gave us a paradox. That's how it was supposed to work. But the bottom line is that if you shoot an arrow at someone or something, yes, you can always go on halving the distance, apparently to infinity, so the arrow never arrives. But we know from experience that sooner or later the arrow will actually hit its target."

I knew he'd got me there. So I switched to fractals.

"Let's compare this to the Mandelbrot set. We've all seen those beautiful coloured representations, the spirals, the ferns, the seahorses, right?"

Charles nodded.

"The key thing is it's infinite. As you go down and down, through the shapes and swirls, it gets smaller and smaller. Take the tiniest part of the tiniest spiral you can see and blow it up, it's the same—or similar. Take a tiny part of that and it scales up. This goes on and on *forever.*"

I looked at him for a surrender! He was chewing it over.

"We can measure across one of the arms or spiral but that is staying in the same physical dimensions. It's when you go into the image that you are traveling in what I think is a new dimension."

"How could you measure that?" he asked.

"I'm not sure you can. I'll give that some thought. But don't you see Charles; I'm saying smaller and smaller in a new direction, that leaves behind existing concepts of measurement. I'm not talking about reducing existing scales until we are smaller than protons or electrons. I mean that those protons and electrons would get smaller and smaller with us. They shrink too. The universe would look the same. Just getting smaller and smaller and smaller, onwards to infinity."

"Not the incredible shrinking man then? OK," he conceded, taking another swig of beer and wiping a line of foam from his lips. He belched loudly. But Charles was no oaf. "This goes beyond the buffer stop of the Planck limit."

"Meaning what?"

"The smallest practical measurement in our universe is the Planck length. Not the Planck constant. It's a figure: the size of an electron, times ten to the minus seventeen. One metre divided by thirty five zeroes or so. Pretty small!" He took another swig. "Nobody knows what use it is but it seems to relate to quantum gravity."

"So an insight into dimensions below the Planck length might have implications for gravity and weightlessness?"

Charles nodded. I felt the hair on my head suddenly stand up on end.

"But it's not just smaller and smaller," I pointed out. "You can travel in both directions: bigger and bigger, as well as smaller and smaller."

"OK, I get it! But what are you going to do with this? You'll have to publish it, at least as a concept paper."

"Somebody will steal it and claim it's their own idea."

"I can help you get it out there, with priority if this checks out," he said, ingenuously.

"That would be great, thanks," I smiled and followed him on down to the bottom of the glass!

But publishing was for the future. My pager went off before we got chance for refill.

For the reader:

You need to see an animated visualization of the beautiful Mandelbrot set. If you haven't done that already, you've missed out on one the math's most amazing tourist destinations!

If you know the Mandelbrot set and have seen it visualized and animated, see it again (you can find examples on the Internet), then turn you attention to the next challenge:

See if you can re-create the visualization I had of the Shrinking Dimension, being very sure not to fall into merely shrinking within the existing measurement frame.

24. Voyage to Arcturus

I am standing on a planet of the Arcturus system. I don't know how I know this, but I do. It is natural to think back to the strange experience at Callanish. Maybe this was the place calling to me and trying to tug me from Earth?

The light is hushed, warm, mysterious. Sounds come, as sacred yet profanely coarse, as rumblings in the belly of an angel. But the most remarkable thing here is the thoughtscape, not the terrain. I *know* I have been here before; I feel there was a girl and the life of a rebel. I came to a bad end, no doubt – but she was worth it, I'm sure! Momentarily, I was relieved to be without a physical form and invisible to the people here, so vivid was the sense of *dèja vu* and the fear of being caught. But of course the antagonists of old were long gone.

There was a moment to speculate about our immortal self: were we the same identical being, moving from identity to identity? Or a kind of collective, an awareness co-operative, which shared knowledge, so that we were all able to access a total past of all beings? Some have suggested that time has no meaning in this context, that past lives are lying all around us, simultaneous, non-linear. But, an essentially logical person, despite my recent right-brain overload, the idea of a linear time line still appealed to me.

As the physical world begins to break up and lose its certainty, my experiences of remote seeing, telekinesis and other-dimensional travel become increasingly common. It takes the least thing to trigger a jump in perception. Sometimes I have only to scrutinize an object closely, whether living or inanimate—a leaf or door handle—and reality begins to tremble and move as it is inspected.

That which is physical—that which I have been conditioned to suppose was physical—has become as insubstantial as a dream, as Buddha always insisted. Suddenly I am faced with existence in a place within that is like a garden, each flower, each seed, each blade or leaf, is a separate world, a universe, a cosmos within a cosmos and I am as a happy humming bee, sipping at the nectars of this new state.

I wished earnestly it could remain permanently but the awesome shifts of perception seem to come and go of their own accord, at times with the force of a quake. Sometimes I can control or initiate it by thinking more deeply, driving consciousness down to deeper and deeper layers of penetration. But most of the time I could do nothing to change what was happening to me.

One thing I did learn is that the kind of thinking necessary to uncover the secret nothing of reality was not intense, not even necessarily aware of itself, but in fact very light. I felt in such moments of exo-spection as delicate as the air disturbed by a migrant butterfly. I was *a feather on the breath of God*, to use Abbess Hildegard of Bingen's memorable metaphor. O that woman, that soul, she that drew the spectacle of the child Jesus being lowered from a flying saucer into the belly of the Virgin Mary. How could she possibly have known such a twentieth-century concept as a flying saucer?

She might have been unlucky and put to death for her Gnostic views and mad visions, were she not so manifestly an incarnation of God in woman. But now, today, we know just how close to the truth she came. In the latter part of the twentieth century we had huge enclaves of people waiting for the flying saucers to return and rescue us; so convinced it will happen in their lifetime, they gasp at every shift of the light, from glowing clouds to reflections of car headlights. To have been aboard an extra-terrestrial spacecraft is for some sad spirits an exalted status, akin once to seeing an apparition of the Virgin Mary.

And why? For all of us the alien world is not "out there". It is that distillation of Totality which congeals just a few inches behind our foreheads!

Slowly the vision of Arcturus begins to fade and I found myself in the Emergency Room.

I was not flying.

A heavy disappointment began to settle over me.

But before I could indulge in self pity, the staff nurse's voice called out for my urgent assistance. I hastened to see what the crisis was – some human's brush with eternity, or a cut finger and too many tears?

That night I lay resting on my bed, attempting to come to terms with what was happening to me. Some of it was just too awesome to comprehend fully. I would need time… there, I said that word: *time*. It creeps in everywhere. As I lay dozing, I passed into an alpha state and turned much of my attention inward. Whether coincidence, or because it was appropriate, I suddenly called to mind the works of the brilliant Russian astrophysicist Nikolai Kozyrev.

A gifted and highly intuitive individual, Kozyrev had expounded an entirely new theory of time. According to him, time is just a form of energy. This could work, because as Paul Davies and John Gribbin tell us, energy is just a concept, rather like time. No-one has ever seen or got hold of energy. We just assume it is there. It explains things.

Similarly, nobody can grasp time. We just see it by the effects it produces. Or, I should say, by the effects we *believe* it produces.

Change is equally critical to time and energy. If nothing changes, nothing moves, neither time nor energy are manifest! It began to sound like a scripture and my excitement knew no bounds. I was gasping at these deep truths and wondered why my mind had never been working at this level in the past.

I realized as I thought about it, this could explain the flowing property of time. Energy must *flow* to manifest itself; it has to go from one place to another, to change, according to laws we call the Laws of Thermo-Dynamics. Energy that isn't moving doesn't exist: it's merely theoretical energy, we call it *potential* energy. I suddenly saw vividly that this could be why time is crucial to flying. If time energy is transformed into the kinetic energy, that could uplift a solid body. Time itself would be transformed and so vanish. But flying would become a reality. Time was the key to flying, exactly as the fairy had said.

What was satisfying was that Kozyrev claimed time had certain properties which could be measured using scientific instruments, like gyroscopes, torsion balances and asymmetrical balances. His conclusion was that time has a density which changes; it is "thin" near the cause end and denser at the effect end of an action. In other words, it appeared to flow between the two, exactly as cause and effect would predict. There was a pattern to the flow of time, which made sense to me, since time without a pattern or matrix would have no reference points.

But also, added Kozyrev, the rate of *flow* was an important property. When time energy flowed through a solid object, it lost weight. The faster the rate of flow, the more weight was lost. Until this moment I had not realized the crucial significance of his theory: *levitation was scientifically possible, it required only an acceleration in the flow of time energy.*

Automatically I called to mind the time the fairy first took me on a trip down into the deeps of time, through quadrillions of years. Now I could see clearly that this rush through an appallingly long time frame gave me the flow of energy I needed to become light and transparent, exactly as had happened that day. Getting that great energy of transformation was crucial to the lightness of being required for flying.

Only one thing about Kozyrev's theory did not satisfy me. Time does not propagate or "spread" like a field force, or energy system, he said; it simply appears *everywhere at once.* That sounded similar to the main property of consciousness, in my view. Perhaps then time was conscious energy and not "field energy"!

I'm sure it was not a coincidence that, before I went to sleep, a new and exciting experience occurred. Lying on my stomach, breathing slowly and deeply, I began to notice a strange sensation. Instead of my nervous system registering the fact that my chest was expanding and contracting, it suddenly began to persuade me that the bed was going up and down, in time with my breathing, like a ship at anchor bobbing on the swell.

It was an extraordinarily satisfying feeling and I simply allowed myself to enjoy the illusion for a few minutes – up and down, up and down, up and down – very hypnotic.

Then, like a bolt from the blue, it came to me that this could be the start of flying. Just the early stages of course but maybe the bed was genuinely beginning to lift with my body? It did feel as if the bed wanted to rise up but kept sinking back. It was back to thoughts about time: the steady rhythm I was creating perhaps brought about an intense need of time energy, which was now transforming into kinetic energy.

In an instant, I knew - it was starting! Flying at last!

But then a Judas thought betrayed me – *if only someone was here to see it!* Instantly, the levitating feeling vanished and everything collapsed to normality. I wanted to kick myself for stupidity. Why could I not simply have accepted what was happening and enjoyed it? Instead I had to clutter up my psychic space with irrelevant and destructive thoughts, more to do with celebrity status than the real end in view.

How stupidly human, indeed.

For the reader:

If you are not aware how much breathing influences consciousness, beware. A state called hyperventilation can do just that. Hyperventilation basically means breathing too much. It is a common response to stress and anxiety and causes many symptoms, including a variety of mental disturbances, from feeling depersonalized, to outright hallucinations. But it can also come on at moments of great excitement, when we say "it takes my breath away".

Chronic hyperventilation is a bad habit and can cause many unpleasant symptoms. It can be corrected with understanding and the correct procedure. Further details are given in the appendix.

25. Transparent Reality

The vision of a distant Arcturian planet was, it seems, only one more step in a major disintegration of reality that had begun. Day by day, as I continued to spend more and more time reaching out into the vast regions of time and space that was my new playground, I caught glimpses of strange dimensions and saw many familar things from a fresh, jarring perspective; and all the while the substantial world I knew seemed less and less reliable!

What was once solid, dependable, safe, suddenly appeared weak and treacherous. It was both thrilling and scary. If you are the type of individual that feels uneasy or fearful, knowing you have forgotten to lock your door, you should experience the sensation of seeing through transparent walls and people! After this happens enough times, nothing will seem real or secure any more.

Without decision or effort, I suddenly found myself working on the problem of time travel. Our main appreciation of Time comes from change. Change can take place in small bytes, such as the heartbeat of a mouse, or in vast aeons, such as the steady decay of a star. Every point in the past was characterized uniquely by an almost infinite number of overlapping cycles of change.

I say almost infinite but in a finite universe, such as the physical reality, there would be a limit. In theory therefore it would be possible, in time ahead, to set up each contributing moment of change, all stacked together in such a way that a moment in the past was recreated exactly: every blade or leaf, every creature, every rock, star and galaxy, all back where they were. It would require huge effort of input. But how it was done was no concern of the time philosopher; merely that it *was* theoretically possible.

Transcendent insights such as these were the probable basis for many scientific breakthroughs. Major shifts of paradigm have usually come from some inspired individual, who is smart enough to know the significance of what he saw in an altered state. It is said that Einstein first vizualized his Special Theory of Relativity by imagining himself riding along on the tip of a ray of light as it shot forward through space. By this stage in my development I had no doubt that he actually *did* ride on the tip of a light beam, in an exalted state of consciousness and intimacy with the mechanics of the universe. Never having met anyone like my fairy mentor, he would suppose it was merely a dream and put it down to a vivid imagination.

At one moment I decided to look intensely at my body, once the old "me". I stared at my left hand. Maybe that was important, because the left side of the body is connected to the right-brain. As we know, the left-brain is quite logical and ordered but the right-brain is more mystical, creatively oriented, with lateral logic. The longer I stared at my own appendage, the more unreal it became. I knew to the bottom of my soul, that this was part of a carbon-oxygen engine but had nothing to do with my conscious self. It began to melt and dissolve. For a moment of alarm, the rest of my body also began to disappear. I calmed myself from the obvious panic: no you are not going insane, Doctor, you are merely carrying out an experiment in perception.

I was finished with so-called reality.

But it was not a time to be smug: I had lost a body! Right, calm once more – think! Cast your awareness round and make contact with it. I found it high up against the outer wall of the hospital. I wished only that I was up there using it as my viewpoint at the time, since I would have achieved my thirty-year dream of flying without wings. But try as I might, I could not see from the body's eyes. I was disappointed yet again by my own ineptness.

The final answer was to lower the body to the floor, which I could do with prodigious effort, and then walk it back into the doctors' mess. As it entered, I thought the thought "That's me." Instantly I snapped back into what I had begun to term the brain identity. All was as normal. Damn! I had now re-imprisoned myself again. Talk about tripping over your own shoelaces!

I tried to repeat the experiment, gazing at my left hand. But nothing would come. After several minutes I gave up and ordered a stiff scotch. It was only afterwards I recognized this event defied any kind of logic. If only I could control processes better than this, it might be fun.

On occasions a strange inner light would flare up and seem to radiate; even friends commented on it, without being quite able to describe what it was they saw. But I knew. It was the refulgence of super-ordinary energies. It was a divine love. Not that I claim conceited divinity in this; I was merely the recipient, like a small glowing light bulb connected to a generator. But I did notice that from week to week I felt more loving, more respectful and more compassionate to everyone I met – even the deadbeats, drunks and motorists who cut me up in traffic! My response to patients became more caring and I found more time to listen to their woes.

One night there seemed to be a real fire storm in my bedroom. I held out my hands and saw rays streaming from the finger tips. It could be just static, I knew. Sailors had long ago described this thunderstorm effect, a blue-ish glow they called St Elmo's Fire. But this was different, because there was nothing in the room to charge my tissues to the necessary voltage. It was the pure energy of the spirit. Perhaps I was showing a temporary halo! When I looked down at my body, I was startled to see a line of blue molten plasma flowing downwards, onto the leg and flying off at the tip of the large toe. It took a few moments to recognize that was my gall bladder meridian, blazing with energies. Was this how the ancient Chinese had come to discover these energy conduits?

After this event, I found myself wonderfully cleansed in body and mind. An extraordinary mental calm settled. Persistent minor aches and pains had disappeared. Restricting emotions like sadness, doubt, anxiety and longing had gone. For the first time in years, I felt free to pursue my own aims, without feeling the deep despair of real love and the residue of grief from the loss of my wife. I would find a just and lovely companion, I knew. It is said in traditional medicine that the gall bladder is the fount of bitterness. Was that what I saw at that moment, flowing outwards and away from my body on the river of light?

But the most fascinating events of all, without doubt, were the contacts with other discarnate beings. There are many out there, of course. Some carry unsettled energies and cause people to shudder at the "ghost"; few can discourse with them freely. I found I could now do so with a second sense I had developed years ago; it had now blossomed further with my new state of being.

I fell into conversation with a melancholic deep-thinking male being who had been with me since Ancient Greece. He explained to me that he had wondered into this universe from some other reality, via a Hellenic temple. This explained something odd for me: countless times I had had a vision of a glowing Greek temple, as if it were on fire. This must have been the moment when the door from one cosmos opened into the other, allowing my friend to enter and then he found he could not get back. Many strange events in human history, supposedly "inexplicable", were probably one of these cross-over shifts.

Not "scientifically-impossible", note. But inexplicable; completely baffling unless you have the right model. Science will tell us nothing about very little, unless it is able to raise its game to these new heights of reality and stop playing around at man-from-sludge molecules. I had forgotten our meeting but this male being remembered of course. We agreed to hang around further and see what other new truths might emerge during my development. He could no more fly than I could, having lived for millennia without a body. Indeed, Earth forms were completely alien to him and disturbed him yet.

I found a group of beings attached to myself who also claimed to have come from some other universe and lost their way home. They were clearly upset, even without a body to express emotions. I have no idea why they should cling to me. Nobody was more lost than I in the known universe, at sea in strange waters, without a map or compass, just an old salty dog skipper to my inexperienced crew.

I dealt with these "entities", as the paranormal psychologists call them, using a method I had known for years. It basically consists of communicating with them telepathically; beings adrift in this way are very nervous and vulnerable and so have to be spoken to with gentleness and compassion. I ask them to describe what beingness or identity they are occupying. Then get them to look at their true cosmic being. That is followed by asking for the date at which they became a conglomerate of beings. It has to be an exact date and they will suddenly split up and go on their own way, laughing and free. This break up will register clearly on a psycho-galvanometer, if you know how to use one properly.

Those are the times when the spirit light is most intense and things begin to dissolve into shimmering mists of great gladness and beauty.

This group dated from many millions of years ago and some kind of planetary explosion had jammed them together. I had been towing them all along, getting their thoughts mixed up in mine. There was some problem disentangling their memories from my own. No wonder I acted confused and out of character at times. This is the stuff of madness, unless you know the facts. I was well aware of multiple personality disorder, of course, and hearing voices in the head—long accepted as a sign of psychosis.

As the greater dimension of our multiple-being expanded before me, I began to understand many things in a new light. As humans we are all composite identities. This was as Gurdieff told us; he spoke of the multiple

"I" and how we switch one to the other, click, click, click, like the dial of a slot machine bandit.

Dear Buddha wrote first of *clearing the fleas* as an essential step towards Nirvana, the bliss of perfect enlightenment. Nevertheless, I felt I had made a sensational discovery, by following my own path to the same conclusion. The human condition was destined to remain one of brutality, wars, insanity, crimes and irrational emotions, until this phenomenon of entities was unravelled and made available to all.

The lost group from another universe were harder to deal with. On recognizing the type of event that had plastered them together, they jostled with excitement, which was quite unpleasant for me. My body went into a cold shock and I shivered uncontrollably, everything dissolved into mist and my body, when I looked down, was quite transparent. Maybe this was the origin of at least some experiences claimed to have been transcendental. A cluster break up could trigger many strange unearthly states.

As they departed, I was told they could now identify their home universe and one or two even said, "Thanks" and "Good luck", which I thought was just about the weirdest application of general courtesy that could be imagined. By this stage I had no problem recognizing the god-like beginnings of so many beings and how we must all, in varying degrees, have fallen from that exalted status described by the fairy's daughter.

When they were gone and I was left alone, a tremendous weight seemed to have been lifted; ninety percent of my subconscious memories had fled with the crowd. I realized how light and misty I felt. My body seemed barely touching the floor and not experiencing the pull of gravity at all. There was a wonderful, airy, fresh feeling and I could feel new energies radiating outwards. I knew at once, without any immediate object of devotion, that it was love.

Later that day many friends, most of them women, commented on my appearance. They noticed my beatific expression and felt the radiation of semi-divine energy. But even some men noticed it, which means it must have been really hugely obvious!

It was time to go back to Skye, to the place I had first met the fairy.

26. The Final Journey North

I play a good bagpipe tune called "The Duke of Roxburgh's Farewell to Blackmount Forest"; I was humming it to myself as I drove up the Blackmount from Bridge of Orchy. Roxburgh Castle is thought by some scholars to be the real Camelot. Malcolm, son of the real Macbeth, was imprisoned there for a time in 1172.

At the top of the hill Blackmount leads out across the wild perilous wastes of Rannoch Moor and on down the Devil's Elbow into Glen Coe, "The Glen of Weeping", so-named for the infamous massacre of 1692. And so to the shores of beautiful Loch Leven and the village with the musical name of Ballachulish (pronounced *balla-hoolish*). A dozen miles further, Ben Nevis was draped in snow lingerie down to a chaste hem at five hundred feet.

To reduce driving strain, I decided against the long but fast drive via Glen Garry, and decided instead to follow the so-called "Road to the Isles" from Fort William to the fishing port of Mallaig. I first traversed this road in my early teens, alone, with scant pocket money and little to eat, sleeping rough. It is not something I would commend to anyone; if the weather is foul you will suffer much and if the weather is good you will suffer more – the Scottish midge is light as dust but with a bite like a lion. I have seen people driven from their tents screaming or cowering indoors in their hotel on a perfectly beautiful summer evening, afraid to go out for fear of the swarms of biting midges.

The road travels west through the wild scenery of Morar. Bonnie Prince Charlie himself was on the run here for weeks after his defeat at Culloden in 1746, sheltered by loyal Highlanders, many of whom paid with their lives for supporting this foppish nancy boy. He too slept rough and must have suffered; and for a short time he would surely have become very tough and fit, before reverting to his bloated aristocratic self-indulgence.

As in all the Highlands, the beauty of the landscape is drenched in a haunting melancholy. There is a kind of time warp. Everywhere one feels the presence of the dead, lost sad souls clinging onto earthly life. Some of them may visit you at night and sing to you in your lodgings. All you will know of it in the morning is the memory of an aching beautiful dream.

Such is the Celtic spirit.

At Arisaig I met the Atlantic Ocean. The silver-white sand here, ground from billions upon billions of sea shells, was one of the stars in the wistful movie *Local Hero*.

From Mallaig, I took the ferry across to Armadale and I was in the southern promontory of Sleat, known sometimes as the garden of Skye. It is the only part of the island which bears any significant number of trees. The woodlands create shelter from the prevailing winds and this allows the cultivation of soft and scented blooms, which abound in many gardens and hedgerows here in the warmer months of the year.

I sped past Armadale Castle, one-time home of the great MacDonald, Lord of the Isles. It is an eighteenth century fake of regency lines and was never finished. The present chief has fallen on harder times and now runs a grand bed and breakfast house a few miles to the north, permitting rich foreigners to dine at the table of the "Lord of the Isles", for a noble price of course.

Back on the usual road I sped west towards Dunvegan. The Cuillin mountains on the left hand rose steeply to the sky, shrouded in dark and agitated clouds. On the opposite side of the road, the land climbed away towards the peak of Roeineval, such a lovely name for the haunt of eagles, an altogether more lonely and secretive place, spurned by the climbers and seldom visited by anyone. After stopping for a pee beside the deserted road, I paused a while before returning to the car, savouring the sweet clean Atlantic air, albeit coming at me quite too much at once!

Suddenly, beside the road, was the fairy. I had not expected him so far from Dunvegan.

"Well met, Doctor," he greeted me.

I must have looked perturbed.

"I sensed your coming and decided to anticipate you," he explained.

"Well, since I cannot travel as you do, you had better come into the car."

This he did, as if nothing was amiss.

"I suppose this might be the first time one of the Old People has ridden in a car?" I said casually, as we drove off.

"Doctor, even as we speak, in cities such as London or New York there may be a dozen or more of the Old People, riding around in cars with their charges."

Duly chastened, I shut up and concentrated on the road. He knew my mind and there was no need to explain what I was doing back on Skye. Little was said on that journey, as I recall. There seemed no value in the empty prattlings of an over-stimulated human, while the fairy remained as laconic and reluctant to start conversations as ever.

But I did make the gesture of deliberately touching him, a statement of silent affinity. I love words but sometimes they cannot do enough.

The touch of two forms, crossing two different planes of reality, was my reward for being bold. His obvious mystery did not intrude; instead I found myself more conscious of a supreme grace, composure and warmth. If he were the Abbot to my erring monk, I was aware only of deep forgiving love and understanding of my sins, errors and conceits.

I dropped him just before the town. It was raining heavily and I felt a little guilty. I tried to protest but he was adamant about not wanting to encounter people.

"Doctor, you must know by now that humans cannot tolerate the presence of mysterious powers or knowledge. For their sake, let me be discreet. This body is just a meta-presence. A little rain is of no concern to me."

And with that he vanished into the dusk.

27. The Engine House Of The Universe

That night I dreamed of being a space agent. Like a cowboy of the ether, I leapt into my craft, pulled the throttle and shot into the deep black intergalactic prairies. I was gripped by the desire to get back out there, among the stars, a free being, able to exist at will in any form or mode. The only element of fantasy was the need for a space craft. A truly free being would need no machine or indeed a body of meat. My former human mind was overwhelmed by the breathtaking scale of what was happening to me, the conscious being. I truly believe that extraordinary spiritual awakenings put great strain upon the body and its workings; it may die.

Next day my mentor and I walked together up the slope to *Biod an Athair*. It was a fine clear day and there was at least one sighting of my power animal, the eagle, come to watch over me. There seemed little to say. The fairy knew my state of mind very well; last minute advice would have been rather contradictory to anything achieved and counter-productive to my present resolved state of mind. With every step up the hill, I felt lighter and lighter as I thought of all that I had learned over the last year and a half from this sublime and gracious being beside me. His companionship had healed me of many wounds, cares and hurts.

I was truly humbled by the curative power of knowledge. Increase of life and zest goes hand in hand with expanded consciousness. I resolved I would encourage others to follow its path all my remaining days as a physician. For this insight alone I felt an immense love towards him.

Still my curiosity would not rest. "Is there truly a *Tir-nan Og*, the Land of the Young, where immortal beings preside?"

"Doctor, you may see it on a clear day from the top of this very hill," he smiled. I suspected an attempt at gentle humor, if not irony. "But this morning," he added, "I have little doubt that you will be able to peer over the horizon in the West and see what lies there for yourself."

I stood poised on the awesome brim. Below me lay the solid familiar Earth and the seas beyond—above me freedom, immortality and undreamed of powers of mind and spirit.

There were no prescribed instructions for this moment. I simply tried to concentrate, calm my fears and shut out the rest of existence. This was between me and the Cosmos; no, between my higher self and my other weak human persona. The secret I felt sure was to just fall forward and do it, just like bungee jumping—which, just for the record, I have always been far too scared to attempt!

There is a Zen parable of the moment of truth which comes to us all. A man is chased by a tiger and scrambles over the edge of a precipice, so that it cannot reach him. He clings to a vine to avoid falling down the precipice to his death, waiting for the danger to pass. But then a little mouse comes and begins nibbling the vine above him. In no time it will gnaw his support to shreds and he will fall. What should he do? Which death to choose, the tiger or the plunge? What is the key to life and death?

Just let go.

To my mind this is identical to the Christian saying, "Only through death shall you find everlasting life."

The same sentiment is most beautifully expressed in Janis Joplin's swan song, *The Rose*: "It's the heart afraid of dying, that never learns to live."

I was not so much afraid I might kill myself with folly but that I would fail at the last and be unable to fly. The very idea of failure was unbearable.

"Stay calm; stay light," I told my trembling self.

"Fear not, Doctor," he said. He must have picked up on my apprehension. "Your own universe awaits you as King."

All of a sudden I was doing it; a sensation of falling. I must have spun around because I quickly lost any sense of up and down or indeed any awareness of the landscape. Instead, I found myself falling into a sea of incredible light, nurturing and warm. The colors changed endlessly. I was lifted up on an ocean of energies, not so much carried by it as becoming part of it. I was in the energy swim. I felt the presence of infinite numbers of beings, so sad, so happy, so endearing, so ardent in striving to be good. I wanted to weep for them all.

It was, of course, a sea of love, aching, sweet and beautiful, like the sum of all the most sublime and honorable feelings we have ever felt, all wrapped up in one emotion.

Once my fluttering nerves began to steady, I found it easy to relax and move around. I grew confident and spread my arms and legs, like a sky diver. In no time at all I was playing *aeroplane* like a kid. Once I had learned that all I had to do was think it, I started to spiral upwards, like a soaring bird. I began wondering where the sea and cliffs were and almost at once the ground appeared, through a gap in the vision which cleared to reveal a fragment of the old reality. I saw the fairy was standing there on the hilltop, silent and still, gazing up towards me.

I made a shift of vision, just in case the stern gaze of a master caused me to falter and fall to my doom. Doom? Who was I kidding! I knew now I could not possibly die; I would never die; death was something which only the body must endure and that was an awesome thought. But still, I didn't want to lose control now with performance nerves. Happy he was in contact, I allowed myself to venture further out, flowing with the tide in what I thought was an upward direction.

I must have moved very fast, without realizing. Looking back, I suddenly saw the whole Earth in the distance, blue, serene and beautiful, exactly as the astronauts have described it. Our planet seemed to pulse with life energies. Perhaps there is a goddess Gaia, after all. No-one who has seen this view could ever doubt that we are all inter-dependent. The fate of one is the fate of all. The very idea of abusive or criminal behaviour towards another is a violence against the perpetrator, against the beloved soul that is the self.

It was in the instant of this realization that I became aware of the presence of wise, loving beings of immensity and power, present all around in realms beyond space. They look down upon us with concern and wonder, aware of our great struggle with meaning, being and experience.

As soon as I was aware of their presence, I felt confused and uncertain. I have trouble with the New Age concept of higher beings regulating our lives from another "plane". If they are so smart, why don't they come down here and *do something*? One answer, of course, is the old conundrum of life and morality, that only by free will may we evolve and learn better ways. Naughty children who are spanked learn little; good behaviour must come from within and cannot be forced.

Simply explaining matters may inculcate the rules of morality but does not create the necessary responsibility for action. To intervene and create "miracles" simply puts Man down further into the mud and causes him to feel lowly and incapable of a meaningful response to life. That is the origin of a vicious manifestation of what passes for divine – that you, the individual, are no good.

Still, there is some evidence for divine intervention, if only because the Earth and its denizens are still there, against almost all odds. Whenever an event has scheduled Earth and Man for doom, something has altered to create a new way forward, with perhaps even more promise. There is even a strong logical core of thinkers and scientists who think this may be the true nature of evolution, not some mindless cold chance selection. Such a callous theory as "social Darwinism" may suit politicians and rapacious acquisitive individuals who want to be able to justify their exploitative and destructive code of conduct. But it does not accord with the spiritual nature of Man, the kinsman of God.

Moreover, it certainly is not intelligent or far-seeing and if taken to its logical conclusion, there would be no storekeepers or taxi drivers to provide for the rich, no voters and no scapegoats for the politicians. What world would be inhabitable if there was no-one there to hear your triumphant shout of "I won! *I own it all!*"

Nevertheless, I felt menaced by these haughty beings who gazed down on our misery. They too were degrades. I sensed a troubled anxiety in their vigil over Earth. It occurred to me they were probably feeling guilty, due to their involvement in the original overthrow of truth and divinity. Then, in one daring thought, I allowed myself to think that maybe they were merely affecting their knowledge and power, trying to hang on to a status long gone. When one moved towards me, as if to greet me, I reacted by withdrawing rapidly. Perhaps it had sensed hostile thoughts.

Too rapidly. I felt a tremendous rush of winds as I fled headlong. There was no logic to this, I knew. Even if I was in the Earth reality, there is no air and no sound in space. Out here, in the dimensions beyond, it made even less sense. Nevertheless, there it was: a distinct sensation of flying through air. I remember just such a feeling when I was under the influence of drugs after having my gall bladder removed. The surgeon had missed one small stone in the lower bile duct and I was in so much pain I was dosed with morphine until the bedclothes and walls began to crawl like worms and snakes.

Next day he decided to extract the stone by passing an endoscope tube down beyond my stomach, slitting open the duodenum at the exit of the bile duct and retrieving the stone with small pliers. There was to be no repeat of the general anaesthetic. The only extra help I got was a light sedative and that, plus the morphine overload, was the final straw that sent me over the cliff edge into raging madness, hurtling through space for several hours.

I wanted to scream as no-one had ever screamed before; but apparently, I merely slept serenely.

It was a terrifying experience and one I vowed never to repeat. Yet here I was, with exactly the same sensation. I was good at ironies!

Like a startled trout running to a new and deeper part of the pool, I shot into yet another dimension and came to rest, trembling. Here everything was free and on a bigger scale. But there were no physical forms of any kind. Instead I seemed to be in some kind of workshop, generating our reality. Blue-prints for the manufacture of worlds, stars and galaxies, not on paper, of course, but in created consciousness format. This stuff was cosmic DNA. Was it also my fifth dimension? Another perpendicular!

Here I, who showed only a masterful ineptitude at mathematics in school, suddenly understood every mathematical formula ever written and could remember them all, even those I had never met. I found the solution to Fermat's Last Theorem in an instant; how could it have taken three centuries to solve, for Heaven's sake! However I noticed that the beautiful abstraction of numbers, which could extend to over a dozen dimensions, remained just that – abstract. There were no realities to match.

I was given another insight, a gift. I knew in that moment it was not possible to argue through all stages and precepts of reason, once and for all, so that from then on mathematics could be reduced to mere rote computation. A newness of creative spirit, of insight, would always be needed to break into new territory.

In other words we are no algorithm and artificial intelligence would never make it to this level, where Einstein danced on the tip of a light beam and Newton had a sudden awareness that apples did not fall but that Earth and apples were attracted towards each other by a mystery force that operates across infinite distances in a void.

I was standing in the place where the Universe was made, I knew that. This was the engine house, the factory of all creation. Strange that none were here to greet me, having made it this far. There could not have been all that many other visitors to this place!

But then, perhaps everyone was present, in a sense, like terminals on a computer network, all accessing the same material but no-one conscious of the other users, even when logged on? I wondered if Plato, in a moment of altered consciousness from wine or herbs, had been here. He argued that true reality was described in an ideal world (literally "ideal" – *from ideas only*), by means of forms which were in a place beyond time and without physical location. These forms gave birth to the physical, imperfect reality which we see.

In a flash I apprehended another clichè truth: that consciousness did indeed create the whole. But more than that, that consciousness was reality. Physical-ness meant nothing of itself. More even than that: consciousness was physical and physical was conscious. The physical universe was alive, there was no other conclusion.

Fred Hoyle, the master astronomer, wrote a story about an interstellar cloud mass that had evolved the ability to think like a human. This is scientifically sound; such a cloud would have billions of charged particles, discharging and re-charging, one against another, just like brain cells. To suggest the chance emergence of conscious thought could never take place in this way would be politically incorrect – modern materialist science-philosophers claim that is just what happened to us! Thought, they say, is just a fluke add-on to the physical brain. One day it was not there, next day thought had arrived. There is no explanation as to how this could possibly come about; scientists just take it as a given.

A conscious universe (or many conscious universes) would mean we needed no wizened beings watching over us from a different plane. Their supposed messages never amount to much anyway, vague abstractions, nothing concrete, nothing you could translate into action for change.

What about the fairy though, was he of this order, just a meddler? Certainly not; his advice was understandable to a scientist, even if shocking, and it could be directly applied in a practical sense. If everyone learned what I had been shown, the world would indeed be free of wars, insanity, crime and violence. We would be back to the game of Being.

The living Cosmos itself is a giant self-regulatory organism, looking after its own – Gaia on a grander scale – perhaps *Ultima* or *Omnia*. We are but corpuscles of light, photons in its ravening energies, quanta in its giant silicon chip. Without us the message is not complete and cannot be decoded. It is an information universe and the word information implies the presence of consciousness. We are thus part of the fabric of existence and the totality of it at the same time. We are the bit, the byte, the chip and the computer, as well as the software and information content. We are also the sentient being sitting at the keyboard, inputting instructions and receiving back data.

It all seemed not merely logical but quite inescapable. But as the pen cannot understand the writing, so we may not separate ourselves from the fabric of existence and take a proper look. The eye cannot see itself, the knife cannot cut itself. *That* was the ultimate trap, the final door to freedom. It followed that the cosmic consciousness wants us all to escape. Everyone get out in the garden while Mama does the chores, shoo!

Five planes up from Earth reality, I hesitated about what to do next. Realizing I had at least to a degree recovered my god head, I knew also there was more, much more, if I wanted to search for it. I could stay out here forever. I needed no body or human life. I was free and could never be restrained, knowing what I now knew!

Then I remembered I had left the car keys in the ignition lock. Damn that human life!

28. First Ending

I woke to find myself lying on my back in the heather, head pointing down the slope. I wasn't hurt and appeared to be undamaged. How had I got here? Cold water was soaking into my clothes and I opened my eyes to find it was almost dusk and raining. I sat up and saw that I was near the road, a long way down from the peak.

The fairy was nowhere in sight.

I stood up and shook myself off and looked at my clothes. They were intact and clean. Therefore I deduced that at least I had not simply rolled down to where I found myself. I was happy about that.

I tried to piece together what had happened here this day.

Had I blacked out and walked down the hill in a trance? Or had I truly flown? There was no questioning the vividness of my experience and feeling of ineffable majesty it brought. But was it real?

It seemed to me it was...

You, reader, must decide for yourself by following your Path to Being. To challenge and overthrow the laws of physics is a personal, very sacred journey back to Being. Follow it if you will. But a word of warning if you do: you will be unable to share your experiences with the world.

Consider it a rule:

If you fly successfully you can tell no-one. You must be prepared for the fact that sad human beings everywhere will mock, scold or deride you. But if you take the path, good luck.

And remember, the end of the road is only the beginning!

29. Second Ending

But we ought to maintain our intellectual integrity and consider a possible alternative ending. The following conversation might have taken place at any stage in my meetings with the fairy, right up to the last, and derailed the whole thing:

"I have trouble with funny magical beings."

"Meaning?" said the fairy, defensively.

"Meaning that you might only be a projection of my own psyche, an image that I empower and give life to, with energies from my own mind."

"A ridiculous idea."

"Not at all. I believe it could be the explanation of many effects, such as ghosts, angels and apparitions."

"If I'm just a projection of your mind, how come I am so much wiser than you?"

"Maybe you're not," I said. "You could be a projection of my higher self, a more fundamental, knowing part of me."

"If it exists, why not just access this store of knowledge directly, instead of such a pantomime?"

"Maybe we humans have lost the power to do that. We need a projection, a metaphor, to talk to, in order to access those hidden areas."

"So how is it that I can fly and you cannot, Doctor?"

"I haven't seen you fly, exactly, though I infer you did at several meetings."

"What if I offer to fly for you now?"

"You wouldn't?"

"Not just to convince a sceptic, no, that's true."

"There, you see? It wouldn't help, anyway. I could imagine you are flying, as I am imagining you standing there right now."

"As you *might* be imagining I am here with you."

"So how do I know?"

"You have thought yourself into a very difficult position, Doctor. I may be real and you are trapped in the vicious mechanics of self-sabotage and defeat that seems to dominate the human mind. Or I may be, as you say, a phantom. Either way, I think, you lose."

"What are we to do?"

"We may try to think of a logical test which will resolve the paradox."

"The obvious one is to call in a third party as a witness or referee."

"No good."

"Why not?"

"As a test of reality, agreement is logically untenable. Many people can hallucinate and only one be lucid and perceiving correctly. I may be real and you are the only human being in existence who can see me. You don't want to fall into the common trap of believing only what the common herd believes, surely? You might abandon your unique and valuable gift in favour of mediocrity and ignorance. If I have judged you aright, Doctor, you wouldn't want that."

"Agreed. But you can't judge me like that. It might be me trying to flatter myself."

He chuckled and shook his head. There was a considerable pause.

"So what are we to do to resolve this; any more ideas?"

"Perhaps you could ask me a question that you know the answer to but I don't," I said lamely, on the spur of the moment.

"O come, Doctor. That's ridiculous. If it were you furnishing my identity and knowledge, you could not impart something that you yourself did not already know."

"You could think of something I didn't consciously know, something I would have to look up in an encyclopaedia or something."

"Doctor, an encyclopaedia is a stream of human knowledge. You could have tapped into it at any stage, subconsciously. You may have heard subliminal details that you think you don't remember, consciously. But the unconscious mind retains everything. Most of your store of knowledge lies in the unconscious and is not directly available to you."

I had to admit this was true. But an idea did occur to me.

"If you are just a projection of the unconscious areas of my mind, and these are not directly perceived, wouldn't I logically be unaware of you too?"

"Ah, a telling point, Doctor!"

"Well?"

"Then we have to ask: *what is the nature of perception?* It's a construct of consciousness and all available philosophical evidence points to the fact that it is independent of outside references. In other words "redness" is not implicit in a red object. A fellow doctor of yours, a Doctor John Locke, raised this question."

"But what if everyone perceives it as red, like a tomato. Doesn't that force the issue of implicitness?"

"The difficulty is in knowing what the other person perceives. We know what *we* mean by the concept of redness but that doesn't mean it is universal."

"But this just brings us back to the three universes!"

"Absolutely! The question then remains: am I in your universe only or in the other persons' universe, or the common reality?"

"I give up."

If the fairy was just an illusion, powered by the author's own thoughts, then of course the entire transformation into a spiritually exalted state could also be an illusion. The doctor might have simply lost his marbles, instead of gaining a certificate in metaphysics.

Mystics have always seemed little better than madmen and women, when viewed from the ordinary human perspective. But their experiences and what they try to tell us as a result may be quite real and the rest of us have missing truths of considerable magnitude. The problem, philosophically (and this goes much deeper down than "scientific proof"), is that there is absolutely no way to know which viewpoint is correct.

Remember that consensus agreement does not make something true, it only makes it *agreed* and that is what the fairy tells us is wrong with ordinary reality (the physical universe). If one person sees a fairy and ten million can see nothing, that does not mean that the lone individual is wrong. It may mean that the one person has a special sensory gift which the others do not possess. And there is no way, scientifically of overthrowing this.

Consider the words of astronomer, mathematician and philosopher, Sir James Hopwood Jeans (1877-1946), written as the impact of relativity and quantum mechanics was shaking science to its core: "The stream of knowledge is heading towards a non-mechanical reality; the universe begins to look more like a great thought than a great machine".

Be humble to be wise.

As an awful warning as to where smugness and rigid intolerance can lead you, consider the story of logical positivism, developed by the "Vienna Circle" during the 1920s and 30s, and later associated with Oxford boffin Sir Alfred Julius Ayer. This philosophical argument was founded on the principle that *unless it can be tested against the objective outer world, any proposition is worthless.*

This arrogant and dismissive standard of authority has been used repeatedly to attack metaphysics and religion. It continues to dominate scientific thinking to this day. But scientists the world over are ignoring the fact that logical positivism was trashed decades ago, when a witty and intelligent individual pointed out that the basic proposition of logical positivism (in italics above) could not be tested against objective experience. In other words logical positivism fails its own defining test and is therefore false!

It's a wonderful joke. But the ferocity with which scientists continue to lambaste and slander those who do not follow this outdated and twisted philosophy is little short of criminal. This is doubly insulting when their own accepted proofs have demonstrated quite clearly that there is no longer such a thing as an objective universe (Bell's Theorem) and that a unique personal universe, operating with its own consistent verifiable rules, is a perfectly valid proposition (Gödel's Theorem).

Would you rather go with the fairy, who is consistent with modern advanced physics and mathematics, or stick with the dinosaurs who tell you other realities are bunk?

I made up my mind long ago, which is why I offer you this little book.

30. Appendix Notes

Chapter 1

Another name for the water horse is the *kelpie*.

The story of dragging the little loch at Suardal is generous poetic license, for the purpose of swift mood setting! Anyone who knows Skye history will know that the loch which was dragged was in fact *Loch nan Dubrachan* along the Armadale to Broadford Road. Moreover the little Church of Chille Chriosd was abandoned long before 1870. However Loch Chille Chriosd was reputed to have its own water horse.

Chapter 2

My account of this (non-fictional) climb was published in detail in *The Great Outdoors* magazine, Sept 1984, pps. 34- 35. Of course I missed out all details of the apparition. You are the first to read it, here.

Chapter 3

The Way of the Shaman, Michael Harner, Harper San Francisco, 1990.

Training of shamans could be pretty rough, as I said. Ostrander and Schroeder cited the practice of selecting Siberian shamans by simply pushing them down through a hole in the winter ice of a river and having him (or her) swim upstream and emerge through another hole several hundred yards away (PSI Psychic Discoveries Behind the Iron Curtain, Shiela Ostrander and Lynn Schroeder, Abacus, London, 1973 p. 254)

Lame Deer: The Life of a Sioux Medicine Man, John Fire and Richard Erdoes, New York: Simon and Schuster, 1972.

The true story of a baby with oesophageal atresia was given to me by Susan Fludd in 1997.

Chapter 4

Tir nan Og means literally the Land of the Young. It is interesting the theme of eternal sweet life on a magical isle beyond the western horizon is used by JRR Tolkein in his Lord of the Rings cycle. Presumably he too knew this Celtic legend.

To learn about Seton Gordon, read Raymond Eagle's important book, *Seton Gordon: The Life and Times of a Highland Gentleman*, Lochar Publishing, Moffat, 1991.

Chapter 5

To hear *McCrimmon's Sweetheart*, try YouTube. Here is an example: http://www.youtube.com/watch?v=UsJAb6aftq8. The piper makes quite good work of the complex ornaments. Bear in mind that with bagpipes, the music can never stop nor the volume of sound be altered. You may be interested to see how pipe composers have solved these little problems!

Chapter 6

Robert A. Monroe ***Journeys out of the Body***, Doubleday, New York, 1973.

Lilly, John C., Man and Dolphins. Doubleday & Company, Garden City, N.Y. 1961.

OBE exercise from Betty Shine, ***Mind Waves***, Bantam Press a division of Transworld Publishers, London 1993.

Chapter 7

On the mathematical validity of a personal universe, see notes for Second Ending on Gödel's theorem. The three universes are discusses at length by Sir Karl Popper (1902-1994). See *Objective Knowledge* (Oxford: Clarendon Press, 1972, 1979); and his contributions to K. R. Popper and J. C. Eccles, ***The Self and Its Brain*** (Berlin, Heidelberg, New York, London: Springer International, 1977).

The Brahan Seer, known in his native Scottish Gaelic as Coinneach Odhar. He is thought to have come from Uig on lands owned by the Seaforths, and to have been a Mackenzie. He is better known, however, for his connections to Brahan Castle near Dingwall, and the Black Isle in Easter Ross. As with Nostradamus most of his prophecies are best known in translation, which can in itself be deceptive.

There are however several strong stories, including his foretelling of the battle of Culloden Muir in 1746, mentioned in chapter 10 of this book. ***"Oh! Drumossie, thy bleak moor shall, ere many generations have passed away, be stained with the best blood of the Highlands. Glad I am that I will not see that day, for it will be a fearful period: heads will be lopped off by the score and no mercy will be shown or quarter given on either side."***

Chapter 8

J W Dunne ***An Experiment With Time***, Papermac, London, 1981 (originally published 1927)

Michael Talbot ***The Holographic Universe***, Harper Perrennial, London, 1992.

Chapter 9

A totem animal is a lifelong symbol, as opposed to a power animal, which may change. It is deeply symbolic and defines certain human characteristics. The use of an eagle's eyes as a "power animal" was well portrayed in the movie Emerald Forest.

Chapter 11

"*The God Particle*" by Nobel laureate for physics Leon Lederman, Mariner Books, New York, 1993.

Chapter 13

Prenatal memories first described by Sadger, Dr J "Preliminary Study Of The Fetus And The Primary Germ", Psychoanalytic Review, July 1941, 28:3. P. 333. He also described the "conception dream".

Contact the **Tunnels of Time** project via my website at: www.scott-mumby.com/tunnels

In his book Between Two Worlds psychiatrist Nandor Fodor interviewed Nijinsky's wife Romala. She had once remarked to Nijinsky ***"It's a shame you cannot see yourself dance!"*** to which Nijinsky replied ***"I do! Always. I am outside. I make myself dance from the outside."***

Chapter 14

"Grok" is from *Stranger In A Strange Land*, Robert Heinlein, Ace Trade edition, New York, 1991.

Shakuntala Devi. On January 24th 1977 before an audience at Southern Methodist University, Dallas, Texas, she beat a Univac 1108 computer; her time was 50 seconds, the computer had taken 62 seconds earlier that same day.

Chapter 15

Much of this chapter is based on a discussion with Prof. Jack Slovak, University of Reno, Nevada. He has a BS physics, an MS physics and MS in electrical engineering.

The story of Joseph of Cupertino is well documented. He is naturally the patron saint of flying!

Chapter 17

Transgression comes from the Latin: trans- across and *gressum* - step. Hence: step over; overstep.

Chapter 18

Seattle Sunday Star on Oct. 29, 1887, in a column by Dr. Henry A. Smith. Do not get confused by the fictional speech created by Ted Perry for a movie in 1972.

The Rowan Tree or Mountain Ash (also known as the "Tree of Life") – genus: ***Sorbus***, is famed for its magical powers. Its berries carry a tiny pentangle, ancient symbol of protection.

A tree really does have an aura, called an L-field! It was first detected by Harold Saxton Burr, who rigged up trees to sensitive electrical detectors. He found that the intensity of the field varied with the seasons. Harold Saxton Burr ***Blueprint for Immortality The electric patterns of life***, Neville Spearman Publishers (The C.W. Daniel Company Ltd.) Saffron Walden, Essex, 1972.

Chapter 19

To "section" a patient refers to various aspects of the (UK) Mental Health Act of 1983. Section 4 of the Act allows an attending doctor to recommend compulsory admission to a psychiatric care unit if, in his or her opinion, the patient is a danger to himself or others. Similar laws apply in other territories.

Chapter 21

The "Christos" Procedure: a Novel ASC Induction Technique by Alastair Iain McIntosh. Psychoenergetic Systems, 1979, Vol. 3, pp. 377–392 0305-7724/79/0301-0061 © Gordon and Breach Science Publishers, Inc., 1979 see also www.AlastairMcIntosh.com

Chapter 22

The Blessed Loch. I am reluctant to give the exact location of this loch; it is best left a secret, lest the hordes find and despoil it. You may write and ask me to tell you where it is, if you think you can persuade me.

Chapter 23

P D Ouspensky ***New Horizons*** (Explorations In Science), Globe Press Books, New York 1990, pp 95–140.

There is some dispute over whether the great pipe tune *The Battle of Vaternish* is the right pibroch. Dates don't fit but common sense says that music historians have somehow muddled the dates. There was no other battle in the Vaternish which would rate this great vaunting piece.

Flatland is a term taken from the book: ***Flatland A romance of Many Dimensions*** (2nd edition 1884) by "A. Square" (actually Edwin A. Abbott 1838- 1926)

Chapter 24

Voyage to Arcturus. Sci-fi fans will probably recognize this as the title of a book by David Lindsay, a strange early venture into space.

Exo-spection is a word I coined – the opposite of introspection; in other words looking outwards.

C.G.Jung, ***Flying Saucers, a modern myth of things seen in the sky***, Ark, 1959, London.(picture between pages 130–131)

According to top physics author professor Paul Davies, energy is a purely theoretical idea introduced to explain certain mechanical and thermodynamic processes. An object moves and we say energy was the reason; a body goes from cold to hot and we say that energy is the reason. But in Davies own words: " We cannot see or touch energy, yet we accept that it really exists because we are so used to discussing it". Paul Davies and John Gribben, ***The Matter Myth***,Viking (Penguin Group), London, 1991.

Most fascinating of all, Kozyrev claims that time has a left-hand twist. This laevo-rotatory effect, as it is known, is absolutely characteristic of life.

Substances with no left-hand turn or with equal right (dextro-rotatory) and left turn are not organic ie. have never been alive. Sheila Ostrander and Lynn Schroeder ***PSI Psychic Discoveries Behind the Iron Curtain***, Abacus, London, 1973, pp 170–179.

Chapter 25

Colin Wilson, G.I. Gurdjieff ***The War Against Sleep***, Aquarian, an imprint of HarperCollins, 1980, London.

Chapter 26

There is much debate over the locality of the King Arthur legend. Around Glastonbury or Tintagel they have had it their own way for far too long. Almost certainly he was based much further north, in the Scottish borders. I will cite just 2 reasons and the interested reader must do further research for themselves:

Of the list of battles Arthur was supposed to have won, none fit south of the border but a surprising number of names are recognizable in the north country.

At the time Arthur was said to have conquered the Welsh, what we now know as Wales did not exist as such, but at that time the Borderlands were called Wales and spoke a Welsh language (remember Arthur was a 5–6th Century ruler, not the Mediaeval figure portrayed by Sir Thomas Mallory).

[Further reading: Michael Wood, ***In Search of the Dark Ages***, Book Club Associates by arrangement with B.B.C. 1981 London].

The title "Lord of the Isles" has been meaningless since the 15th Century, when rebellious John MacDonald the IVth Lord had his title stripped by the crown.

Chapter 27

The Engine House of the Universe: the title for this chapter is taken from a quote by John C. Lilly.

Vermification is a well-known side effect of too much morphine: the surroundings begin to turn into wriggling shapes, as if made of worms.

Fred Hoyle *The Black Cloud*, Buccaneer Books, 1993 (reprint).

Chapter 29

Godel's Theorems:

1. Any logical system which is complex enough to include at least simple arithmetic, can express true assertions which cannot be deduced from its axioms.
2. Axioms within such a system, with or without additional truths, cannot be shown in advance to be free from hidden contradictions.

Kurt Gödel from Austria was mathematician and logician at Princeton in 1931, when he showed that mathematical statements existed for which no external reference of validity exists. It was damaging enough but, as Professor Roger Penrose points out, what Gödel demonstrated was widely applicable to all science.

But Penrose goes further and declares that "in establishing his theorem, he (Gödel) initiated a major step forward in the philosophy of the mind". Gödel showed that "human intuition and insight cannot be reduced to any set of rules." Nothing could be tested objectively, without, in effect self-referencing, which was in ordinary ways of thinking, a waste of time!

One can create any universe at will, complete with its own set of coherent axioms, and this cannot be logically disputed from some exterior system of rules or order. (Penrose R. *"Shadows of the Mind"*, Oxford University Press, London, 1994, pp 64-65)

Bell's Theorem:

Professor Henry Stapp, a physicist at Berkeley has called this the most important discovery in the history of science. In his words: "If the statistical predictions of quantum theory are true, an objective universe is incompatible with the law of local causes." Put in everyday language, it means if we have two events instantaneously influencing each other, then the idea of an objective world is out of the question. It's all in the mind!

The theorem was first proposed in 1964 by the physicist John S. Bell was first confirmed by experiment in 1972 by Professor John Clauser at Berkeley and later Alain Aspect in Paris in 1982. This was the end of science as we know it.

Logical Positivism

Developed by the so-called "Vienna Circle" during the 1920s and 30s, this philosophy was developed in an attempt to systematize empiricism in light of developments in math and philosophy. The term itself was first used by Albert Blumberg and Herbert Feigl in 1931.

For logical positivists, the entire discipline of philosophy was centered on one task: to clarify the meanings of concepts and ideas. This, in turn, led them to inquire just what "meaning" was and what sorts of statements really did have any "meaning" in the first place.

According to logical positivism, there are only two sorts of statements which have meaning. The first encompassed necessary truths of logic, mathematics and ordinary language. The second encompassed empirical propositions about the world around us and which were not necessary truths - instead, they could only be regarded as "true" with greater or lesser probability.

The most famous doctrine of logical positivism is its verifiability principle, developed as a means for identifying the second of the above two types of statements. According to this principle, the validity and meaning of any proposition is dependent upon whether or not it can be verified. Thus, a statement which cannot be verified is held to be automatically invalid and meaningless.

This became for many people a basis for attack on metaphysics, theology and religion because those systems of thought make many statements which cannot, in principle, be verified in any way. These propositions might qualify as expressions of one's emotional state, at best - but nothing else.

Sir Alfred Julius Ayer was an English philosopher who developed key features of logical positivism. His book *Language, Truth, and Logic* (1936) is one of the most influential philosophy books in the 20th century, addressing questions of reality, perception, knowledge and meaning.

But as I said in the story, logical positivism fails its own defining test! Nothing to do with a standard, objective and immutable universe stands up to scrutiny, despite the intolerant pomposity of writers like Richard Dawkins.

The *only* defining parameter of the universe and what is "real" is what we perceive and choose to believe. We could all fly tomorrow, if only we could get our heads round this wonderful truth.

THE END

Websites

You can get connected with Keith Scott-Mumby and keep updated on any further thoughts about magical flying at:

www.SecretsTheFairyToldMe.com

For Dr. Keith's medical writings, start out at:

www.Alternative-Doctor.com